OCEAN LIFE
ENCYCLOPEDIA

OCEAN LIFE
ENCYCLOPEDIA

Jinny Johnson

First published in North America by Mondo Publishing
980 Avenue of the Americas
New York, NY 10018

ISBN: 1-59336-859-3
Library of Congress Cataloging-in-Publication Data
available on request.

Originated in Hong Kong by Modern Age
Printed and bound in China by
SNP Leefung Printers Limited

Publisher: Richard Green
Commissioning editor: Claudia Martin
Art direction: Ivo Marloh
Design and editorial: Tall Tree Ltd.
Designers: Ed Simkins, Ben Ruocco,
Jonathan Vipond, and Siân Williams
Editors: Jon Richards and Catherine Saunders
Production: Nikki Ingram

Contents

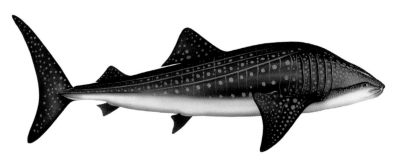

Introduction

Life has thrived in the ocean for over four billion years—far longer than on land. In fact, more of the land on this planet is under water than is above it. From warm tropical waters to icy polar seas, from colorful coral reefs to the lightless depths, oceans cover two-thirds of the earth's surface. But while humans have mapped every continent, the ocean is largely a fascinating world still waiting to be explored.

Yellowfin tuna live in the Atlantic and Pacific oceans. They grow to be about 6 feet (1.8 m) long and weigh about 450 pounds (200 kg).

Animals that spend their lives under and around the water have adapted in a variety of ways to survive the challenges of ocean life. All living creatures need oxygen, but the molecules of oxygen in the oceans are dissolved in water. Fish, sharks, and many other marine animals extract dissolved oxygen from water as it flows past their gills. Mammals, such as whales and seals, don't have gills, so they return to the surface to breathe.

No sunlight penetrates the deepest parts of the ocean. Below 3,300 feet (990 meters), the water is completely dark, and no plants grow. But there is life here, too. Fish and other creatures hunt each other and scavenge food that drifts down from the sunlit waters above. Some fish even have chemicals in their bodies that make them glow in the dark.

Animals that live on the seashore face crashing waves and changing tides, which can cover them with water, sweep them away, or leave them exposed. They have developed a variety of means of survival, such as attaching themselves to rocks or burrowing into the sand.

Penguins slip and slide as they waddle over the Antarctic ice. Emperor penguins often lie down on their bellies and toboggan instead.

How to use this book

This encyclopedia of ocean animals is divided into two chapters: "The Oceans" and "The Seashore." Each chapter contains both catalog pages, which illustrate and give facts about many different species, and focus pages, which look in more detail at particularly interesting animals, such as sharks or penguins. There are also pages that examine the different aquatic ecosystems, such as the seashore, the deep ocean, and coral reefs.

Weedy seadragon

Size: 18 in (47 cm)
Range: coastal waters of southern Australia
Scientific name: *Phyllopteryx taeniolatus*

Habitat
Habitat symbols show where the species or animal family lives. A key appears below.

Size
The approximate size of the animal is given in imperial and metric measurements.

Range
This lists the areas of the world in which the species is found.

Scientific name
Most species of animals have a common name, such as the "weedy seadragon," which can vary from place to place. All species have a scientific or Latin-based name, which never changes. It is shown in *italics*.

Key to habitat symbols

Coral reef

Fresh water
includes rivers, lakes, lagoons, marshes, floodplains, riverbanks, and underground water in caves.

Oceanic
includes mudflats, shores, cliffs, islands, and tidal areas.

Coast
includes mudflats, shores, cliffs, islands, and tidal areas.

Deep sea

Coastal waters
includes estuaries and the seabed.

Polar
includes Antarctic and Arctic regions, pack ice, and ice floes.

The oceans

Extraterrestrials visiting our world for the first time might be puzzled as to why we call our planet "Earth." From space, our planet looks blue, with over two-thirds of its surface covered in ocean. Planet "Ocean" would be a more accurate name for our world. As humans, we have a land-centered view of the planet because, for the most part, we live on solid ground.

Oceans can be warm or cold depending on their location in the world. Tourists flock to tropical beaches where warm blue water laps the shore (below) while the cold polar seas are dotted with icebergs (above).

A false-color 3D computer image of the ocean floor. The land is shown in black. The four true oceans of the world—Atlantic, Arctic, Indian, and Pacific can be seen.

Oceans

The ocean covers 71 percent of the planet. The continents divide this expanse of water into four separate oceans—the Pacific Ocean, the Atlantic Ocean, the Indian Ocean, and the Arctic Ocean. The Pacific Ocean is by far the largest. It contains about the same amount of water as the other three oceans combined. Some people include the Southern Ocean around Antarctica, but it is not a true ocean: it is an extension of the Pacific, Atlantic, and Indian oceans.

In this relief map of Europe, the Mediterranean Sea is seen from the west. The narrow Strait of Gibraltar at the bottom right of the picture connects the Mediterranean Sea to the Atlantic Ocean.

Seas

"Sea" is another name we use for ocean. But "sea" also describes part of an ocean. For example, the Caribbean Sea is part of the Atlantic Ocean, and the Arabian Sea lies in the Indian Ocean. Some seas, such as the Mediterranean Sea and the Red Sea, are almost completely surrounded by land. They are connected to a nearby ocean by a narrow passage called a strait. "Gulf" is an alternative word for a sea, as in the Gulf of Mexico or the Persian Gulf.

Watery world

More than 97 percent of the world's water is found in the oceans. As fresh water runs over rocks and along rivers, it picks up mineral salts from the soil. Eventually these salts are carried into the sea. Over billions of years, enough salt has been washed into the ocean to make the water salty.

Moving water

Water on Earth is constantly on the move. Water from the surface of the oceans evaporates and enters the air, where it forms clouds. The clouds are blown across the ocean and return water to the sea when it rains, hails, or snows. Some clouds unload their water over land and so fill lakes and rivers and soak the ground. Soil and underground rocks take up plenty of water almost like a sponge. The water running off the land feeds streams, lakes, and rivers. Most of this water eventually returns to the sea at river estuaries.

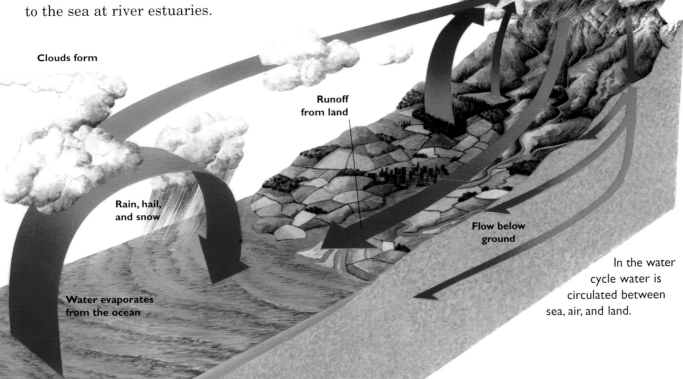

Some clouds are blown over land or form over land

Clouds form

Rain, hail, and snow

Runoff from land

Flow below ground

Water evaporates from the ocean

In the water cycle water is circulated between sea, air, and land.

Ocean life

Life manages to survive in all parts of the ocean, but the most highly populated waters are those near the surface. Here plenty of light penetrates to about 330 feet (100 m) and plant plankton thrive. These microscopic plants are eaten by animal plankton—tiny animals that drift in surface waters. Animal plankton includes two types of creatures, those that remain plankton all their lives and those that only drift with the plankton while they are larvae. Eventually they develop into adult animals, such as crabs and barnacles, with many different lifestyles.

Among the larger creatures in the oceans there are at least 160,000 species of **invertebrates**, such as sponges, muscles, and squid.

What is a fish?

Fish were the first vertebrates—animals with backbones—to live on Earth. The earliest fish lived about 500 million years ago.

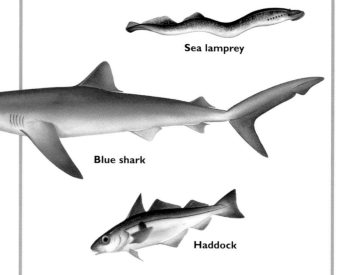

Sea lamprey

Blue shark

Haddock

Structure of a fish

There are three main groups of fish. The most primitive group includes the lampreys and hagfish. These fishlike animals have no jaws, only a suckerlike mouth. The second group includes all the sharks and rays. These are known as cartilaginous fish because their skeletons are made of a gristly substance called cartilage. The third, and largest, group contains the bony fish, which have skeletons made of bone.

What is an invertebrate?

Crab

An invertebrate is an animal without a backbone—creatures such as crabs, worms, insects, and spiders are all invertebrates. There are invertebrates on land, in the sea, in fresh water, and in the air. These animals have a range of lifestyles and feeding habits.

Arthropods

Arthropods are the largest group of invertebrates and include creatures such as insects, spiders, and crabs. Arthropods have a hard external skeleton, called an exoskeleton, which protects the soft body within.

Nautilus

Echinoderms

There are four main groups of echinoderms—brittle stars, sea stars, sea cucumbers, and sea urchins and sand dollars. Most move around using tiny stilts called tube feet.

Flower urchin

Mollusks

The three main groups of mollusks are the gastropods—creatures such as snails; the bivalves—clams, scallops, and mussels; and cephalopods—squid, cuttlefish, octopuses, and nautiluses.

What is a mammal?

Blue whale

Mammals are a very diverse group of animals, but they all have certain things in common. They are warm-blooded, have lungs to breathe in air, have relatively large brains, and have a bony skeleton to support their bodies.

Mammal birth

Most mammals give birth to live young. In the majority of mammals, known as eutherians, the babies grow inside the mother's womb until they are born.

Of the vertebrates, **fish** are the most common. There are at least 14,000 different kinds of fish, from tiny infantfish, which are ¼ inch (7 mm) long, to the whale shark, which grows 40 to 60 feet (12–18 m) long.

There are a few marine **reptiles**, including sea snakes, turtles, and one lizard—the marine iguana. Many types of **birds**, such as gannets, gulls, and petrels, depend on the sea for their food, and nest on shores and sea cliffs. Other birds, such as penguins, are expert swimmers.

A number of **mammals**, such as whales and seals, have adapted to life in the sea. More than 80 species of whales live their whole lives in the sea and cannot survive out of it. Seals spend much of their lives in the sea, but come to land to breed and give birth.

What is a reptile?

Saltwater crocodile

Reptiles are vertebrate animals. Their bodies are covered in tough waterproof scales. Most reptiles live on land, but turtles and some snakes live in water, and crocodiles spend time both in water and on land.

Kinds of reptiles

Four groups of reptiles survive today. Turtles and tortoises have short, broad bodies, enclosed by a bony shell. Crocodiles and alligators are hunters and the largest living reptiles. The third group includes lizards and snakes. The fourth group are tuatuaras.

Eastern box turtle

Dark green whipsnake

What is a bird?

A typical bird has a strong but light body, two legs, and a pair of wings. The wings are, in fact, modified forelimbs. All birds are covered with feathers and are the only creatures to have feathers. The feathers are made of keratin, a protein that also makes up the scales on reptiles and the hair and nails of humans and other mammals.

Bird anatomy

Strong wings keep the body in the air, and its tail feathers are spread to help it steer during flight. All birds have wings, beaks, and claws that are shaped for their particular lifestyle.

Common tern

The Oceans

The vast areas of open ocean far from land are a mystery to most people, but beneath the surface, a range of creatures from jellyfish to whales find their home.

Life is less abundant in the open ocean than in waters nearer land. Shallow coastal seas are rich in nutrients washed down from the land, and this encourages the growth of plankton, the basis of all ocean life. In the open ocean, there are fewer nutrients and, therefore, less plankton. However, the open sea experiences less dramatic change than the coast, which is covered and uncovered by tides.

Creatures living in the open sea have nowhere to hide, so they need other ways of protecting themselves. Some, such as jellyfish, have stinging cells on their tentacles, which help them to defend themselves against enemies as well as to catch prey. Larger fish, such as tuna and marlin, have few enemies. They are high-speed swimmers, able to travel huge distances to find their prey.

Many small fish, such as bluestripe snappers, gather in huge schools and find safety in numbers.

Sargassumfish

13

Sharks

Sharks and their relatives are all cartilaginous fish—they have skeletons made of cartilage rather than bone. In total there are about 300 species of shark, and they all live in the sea. Most of them are active hunters, equipped with sharp-edged teeth in both their upper and lower jaws. A few of the largest, such as the whale shark, are not hunters. Instead, they use rakers on their gills to filter small creatures from the water.

Short fin mako shark

Short fin mako shark

A powerful fish with a slender body and a pointed head, the mako is a fast-swimming, aggressive hunter. It usually feeds on surface-living fish, such as tuna and mackerel. The female mako gives birth to live young, which develop inside her body.

Size: 6½–13 ft (2–4 m)
Range: Atlantic, Pacific, and Indian oceans
Scientific name: *Isurus oxyrinchus*

Smooth hammerhead shark

This shark has one eye and one nostril on either side of its elongated head. This spacing of its features may improve its sight and sense of smell. It is known to attack people.

Smooth hammerhead shark

Size: 14 ft (4.3 m)
Range: all oceans
Scientific name: *Sphyrna zygaena*

Sandy dogfish

A small shark, the sandy dogfish lives on sandy and muddy seafloors, where it feeds on fish and bottom-living invertebrates. The female's eggs are laid in hard cases, which lodge among seaweed or other objects. The young dogfish hatch 5 to 11 months later and are about 4 inches (10 cm) long.

Sandy dogfish

Size: 23–40 in (60–100 cm)
Range: north Atlantic Ocean
Scientific name: *Scyliorhinus canicula*

White shark

A large, aggressive hunter equipped with jagged triangular teeth, the white shark (also called the great white) kills seals, dolphins, and even other sharks. It also feeds on dead animals and waste. White sharks have been involved in a number of attacks on humans.

Size: 19½ ft (6 m)
Range: Atlantic, Pacific, and Indian oceans
Scientific name: *Carcharodon carcharias*

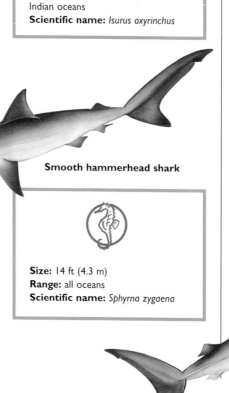

White shark

Basking shark

The basking shark is the second-largest living species of fish. It shares the streamlined body shape of other sharks but has extra-large gill slits. It feeds on plankton, which it sieves from the water using the comblike bristles on its gill arches. The shark swims with its mouth open, takes in vast quantities of water and plankton, and filters them through the gill slits. Basking sharks often float sluggishly at the surface of the water. Little is known of their breeding habits, but the basking shark's eggs are believed to develop inside its body, hatching as they are expelled. The young sharks are about 5 feet (1.5 m) long at birth.

Whale shark

Whale shark

The whale shark is the biggest of all fish. Despite its size, it is not a fierce hunter. It eats tiny animal plankton, which it filters from the water. The shark opens its mouth and takes in a rush of water, which contains lots of small creatures. The water flows out through the gill slits, leaving the plankton in the shark's mouth.

Size: up to 60 ft (18 m)
Range: all oceans
Scientific name: *Rhincodon typus*

Bull shark

The bull shark has a chunky body, with its first dorsal fin placed well forward. Normally quite slow-moving, it is usually found in shallow water and regularly swims into rivers. Bull sharks eat a wide range of fish, including rays and small sharks, and they also eat shrimps, crabs, and sea-urchins. The female produces live young, generally from May to July in salty inshore waters.

Thresher shark

The thresher's tail is as long as the rest of its body. It feeds mainly on schooling fish and, alone or in pairs, uses its tail to herd the fish into a compact mass, which is easier prey. A thresher may also strike and stun individual fish with its tail. Threshers sometimes hunt in coastal waters, particularly in summer. Females give birth to litters of 2 to 4 fully formed young, which may be as long as 5 feet (1.5 m) at birth. In Australia, the thresher shark is known by different scientific names—*Alopias caudatus* and *Alopias grayi*.

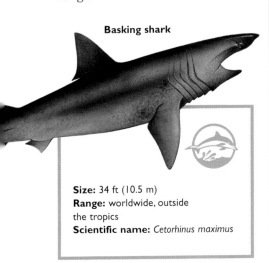

Basking shark

Size: 34 ft (10.5 m)
Range: worldwide, outside the tropics
Scientific name: *Cetorhinus maximus*

Size: 8¼–11½ ft (2.5–3.5 m)
Range: west Atlantic Ocean—North Carolina to south Brazil
Scientific name: *Carcharhinus leucas*

Bull shark

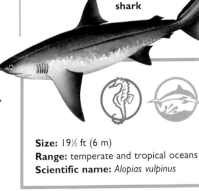

Thresher shark

Size: 19½ ft (6 m)
Range: temperate and tropical oceans
Scientific name: *Alopias vulpinus*

Bluntnose six-gilled shark

A long-bodied shark, with a long tail fin and one dorsal fin near the tail, this species has six pairs of gills. Although sluggish, it is powerful and feeds on a wide range of bottom-living fish, such as rays, as well as crustaceans. It is believed to mate in the spring. The eggs develop and hatch inside the mother, and the young are 18 to 24 inches (46 to 61 cm) long when they are born. There are often 40 or more in a litter.

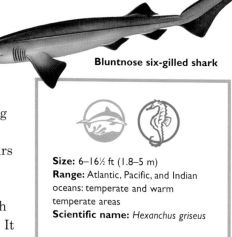

Bluntnose six-gilled shark

Size: 6–16½ ft (1.8–5 m)
Range: Atlantic, Pacific, and Indian oceans: temperate and warm temperate areas
Scientific name: *Hexanchus griseus*

Monkfish

The monkfish's broad pectoral fins resemble those of a ray. However, the gills positioned at the sides, the mouth at the front of its head, and well-developed dorsal fins reveal it to be a true shark. The monkfish lies almost buried in sand or mud much of the time, but it can swim well. It feeds on bottom-dwelling fish, and gives birth to live young, in litters of 9 to 20, from eggs that develop and hatch inside the mother.

Size: 6 ft (1.8 m)
Range: North Sea; east Atlantic Ocean: Scotland to North Africa and Canary Islands; Mediterranean Sea
Scientific name: *Squatina squatina*

Common saw shark

The common saw shark is one of five species of saw shark. It has a distinctive snout with sharp, alternately large and small teeth along each side. It moves around very little, probing in the mud of the seabed for food, which it detects with the aid of sensitive barbels on its snout. Its young are born well-developed, but their teeth are encased in skin and do not appear until after birth.

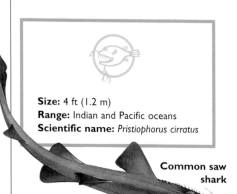

Common saw shark

Size: 4 ft (1.2 m)
Range: Indian and Pacific oceans
Scientific name: *Pristiophorus cirratus*

Sand tiger

The sand tiger is a predatory shark. It has long, pointed teeth and lives in shallow water. The female gives birth to two young, which develop inside her body for 12 months and are about 39 inches (1 m) long at birth. The sandtiger is closely related to the raggedtooth shark.

Sand tiger

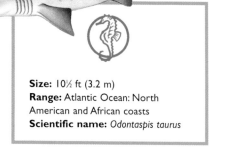

Size: 10½ ft (3.2 m)
Range: Atlantic Ocean: North American and African coasts
Scientific name: *Odontaspis taurus*

Blue shark

The blue shark has long pectoral fins, a pointed snout, and a bright color. It feeds on a range of surface-dwelling fish, squid, and waste thrown from fishing boats. Females give birth to litters of up to 60 live young. Blue sharks make regular migrations to warmer waters in the winter months.

Size: 9–12½ ft (2.7–3.8 m)
Range: Atlantic, Pacific, and Indian oceans: temperate and tropical areas
Scientific name: *Prionace glauca*

Blue shark

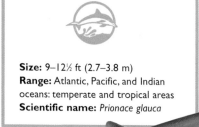

Spiny dogfish

Easily identified by the large spine in front of each dorsal fin, the spiny dogfish, or spurdog, has a long, slender body; a pointed snout; and large eyes. Spiny dogfish move in large schools, often of only one sex. They bear live young, which develop for 18 to 22 months. From three to 11 young are born at any one time.

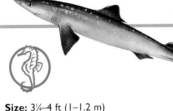

Spiny dogfish

Size: 3¼–4 ft (1–1.2 m)
Range: north Atlantic Ocean: coasts of Norway, Britain to North Africa, Greenland to Florida; Mediterranean Sea; north Pacific Ocean
Scientific name: *Squalus acanthias*

Porbeagle

The porbeagle is a heavy-bodied, fast-swimming shark with five gills. Eggs hatch inside the females and stay there for a short time before she gives birth to litters of one to five fully formed young. The salmon shark (*Lamna ditropis*) of the Pacific, is similar to the porbeagle in its appearance and habits.

Size: 6–9¾ ft (1.8–3 m)
Range: north Atlantic Ocean: Newfoundland, south to South Carolina, Iceland, south to north Africa; Mediterranean Sea
Scientific name: *Lamna nasus*

Port Jackson shark

The Port Jackson shark has the large, heavy head; bulging forehead; and ridge over each eye that are typical of bullhead sharks. Other features include the dark-brown markings encircling its grayish-brown body and the stout spines in front of each dorsal fin. This shark feeds mostly at night. Its small mouth has sharp, pointed teeth at the front and, farther back, broader crushing teeth, which are perfect for eating hardshelled mollusks and crustaceans. Year after year, these sharks are believed to migrate to the same shallow coral reef areas to breed.

Size: 21 ft (6.4 m)
Range: north Atlantic Ocean: inside Arctic Circle, south to Gulf of Maine and Britain
Scientific name: *Somniosus microcephalus*

Size: up to 5 ft (1.5 m)
Range: south Pacific Ocean; Southern Ocean: coasts of Australia from south Queensland to Western Australia
Scientific name: *Heterodontus portusjacksoni*

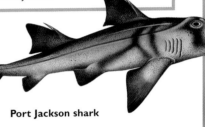

Port Jackson shark

Greenland shark

The Greenland shark is the giant of its group, but unlike other Atlantic spiny sharks, it has small dorsal fins with no spines in front of them. It seems to be a slow-moving bottom-dweller, but it will come to the surface in search of food, particularly during the winter. It preys on many kinds of fish, both surface- and bottom-living, and also feeds on mollusks, crustaceans, and squid, and sometimes on seals, porpoises, and seabirds. Female Greenland sharks give birth to live young from eggs that develop and hatch inside the mother's body.

Porbeagle

Greenland shark

Sharks

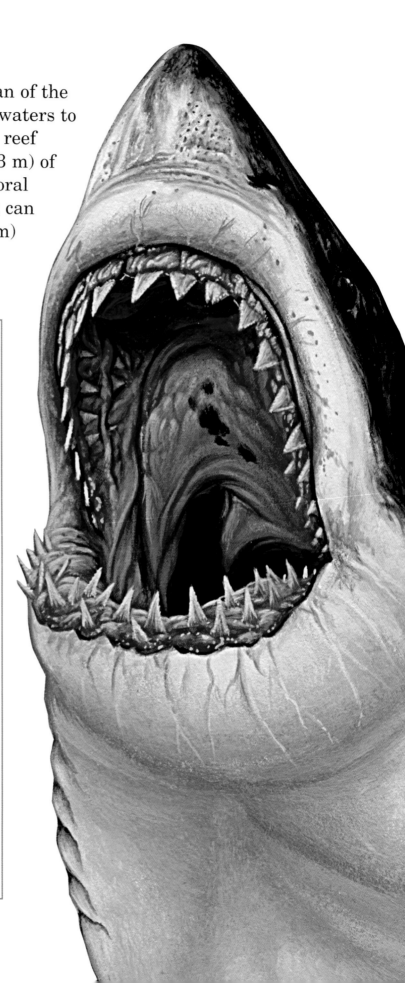

Sharks are found in every ocean of the world—from shallow coastal waters to the deepest oceans. The blacktip reef shark can swim in just 1 foot (0.3 m) of water in order to hunt above a coral reef, while the Portuguese shark can be found more than 2 miles (3 km) down, making it one of the deepest-living sharks.

Teeth

Shark teeth come in many shapes and sizes. The teeth of each shark are shaped to help it catch and eat its prey quickly and easily.

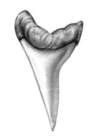

The teeth of the mako shark are long, thin, and very sharp. They are specially designed to catch slippery fish.

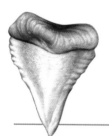

The bronze whaler shark has narrow, jagged-edged teeth that are perfect for catching and gripping its prey.

Horn sharks have pointed teeth (shown) at the front to catch small fish, and large, flat teeth at the back to crush sea urchins.

Breathing underwater

Sharks and other fish take in oxygen from the sea through their
gills. Blood vessels carry oxygen-rich blood from the gills to the
rest of the body. Many hunting sharks must keep swimming to
pass the oxygen-rich water over their gills. If they stop, they
will sink and drown. Some bottom-dwelling sharks are able
to rest on the seabed by pumping water over their gills.

Skin

Sharks have tiny teeth all
over their skin. The teeth
guide the water over the shark's
body to help it slide through the
sea. Modern swimsuit fabrics have
imitation "sharkskin teeth" to
help swimmers move faster.

The skin teeth of a
shark point backward,
making it as streamlined
as possible.

Hagfish, lampreys, skates, and rays

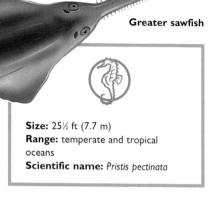

Greater sawfish

Size: 25½ ft (7.7 m)
Range: temperate and tropical oceans
Scientific name: *Pristis pectinata*

Hagfish and lampreys are primitive, fishlike animals that have no true jaws. Hagfish have a slitlike mouth surrounded by small tentacles. Lampreys have a sucking disk for feeding on the blood of other creatures. All hagfish live in the sea, but there are some fresh-water lampreys.

Skates and rays are related to sharks. There are 456 species of skate and ray, and most of them live in warm tropical seas.

Greater sawfish

Also known as the smalltooth, the greater sawfish has a long, sawlike snout. Each side is studded with 24 or more large teeth. The sawfish lives on the sea bed in shallow water and uses its saw to dig in the sand and mud for small invertebrates to eat. It may also swim into a school of fish and lash its saw from side to side to stun prey.

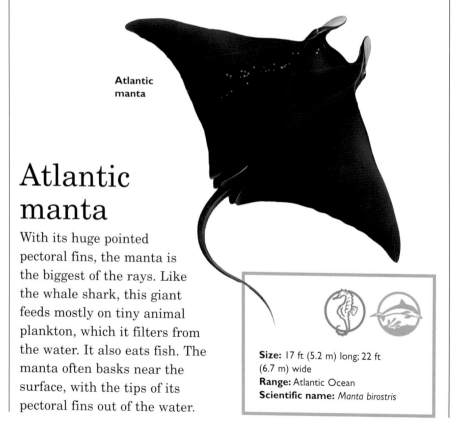

Atlantic manta

Atlantic manta

With its huge pointed pectoral fins, the manta is the biggest of the rays. Like the whale shark, this giant feeds mostly on tiny animal plankton, which it filters from the water. It also eats fish. The manta often basks near the surface, with the tips of its pectoral fins out of the water.

Size: 17 ft (5.2 m) long; 22 ft (6.7 m) wide
Range: Atlantic Ocean
Scientific name: *Manta birostris*

Atlantic hagfish

The hagfish has no jaws, just a slitlike mouth surrounded by small tentacles. It feeds on crustaceans, but it also eats dead and dying fish. Using its toothed tongue, the hagfish bores into the prey's body and eats its flesh.

Atlantic hagfish

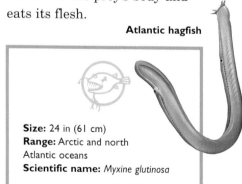

Size: 24 in (61 cm)
Range: Arctic and north Atlantic oceans
Scientific name: *Myxine glutinosa*

Sea lamprey

The adult sea lamprey is a blood-feeding parasite. It uses its mouth to attach itself to its prey so firmly that it is almost impossible to remove. A special substance in its mouth keeps the prey's blood flowing so the lamprey can feed. The host often dies from blood loss.

Sea lamprey

Size: 35½ in (90 cm)
Range: Mediterranean Sea and Atlantic Ocean; larvae live in fresh water
Scientific name: *Petromyzon marinus*

Atlantic guitarfish

A common fish along the western north Atlantic coast and Gulf of Mexico, the guitarfish's body shape is a cross between sharks and rays. It is long and rounded, with well-developed dorsal fins, but the pectoral fins are enlarged, and the gills are on the underside of its body. It is a bottom-dweller and feeds on crustaceans, mollusks, and small fish.

Size: 30 in (76 cm)
Range: western north Atlantic Ocean: North Carolina to Gulf of Mexico
Scientific name: *Rhinobatus lentiginosus*

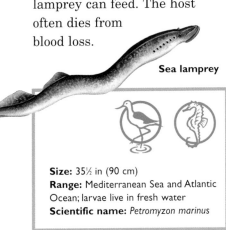

Atlantic guitarfish

Skate

Large numbers of skate are caught for food. Skates live in waters 100 to 2,000 feet (30 to 600 m) deep; only young fishes are found in the shallower part of this range. The skate has a flat body, broad pectoral fins, and a tiny tail. There are small spines on the tail and on the underside of the body. Adult females also have spines on the front edge of the body, while males have spines on their backs. Skates are bottom-dwellers—they eat fish, crabs, lobsters, and octopuses. Their eggs are deposited on the seabed and are covered in horny capsules that have long tips at each corner. Hatchlings are about 8 inches (21 cm) long.

Size: 6 ft (1.8 m)
Range: Atlantic Ocean: Scotland to South Africa, Nova Scotia to North Carolina; Mediterranean Sea
Scientific name:
Torpedo nobiliana

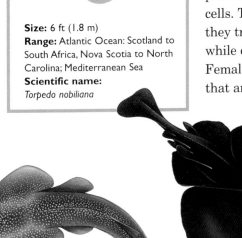

Skate

Size: 8 ft (2.4 m)
Range: east Atlantic Ocean: Arctic Ocean to Madeira; Mediterranean Sea
Scientific name: *Raja batis*

Atlantic torpedo

Torpedo rays can give electric shocks of 70 to 220 volts, which is enough power to kill or stun a fish or to throw a human to the ground. The electric discharges of these fish are produced by modified muscle cells. Torpedos eat fish, which they trap in their pectoral fins while delivering the shock. Females produce live young that are about 9 inches (25 cm) long when they are born.

Atlantic torpedo

Tarpon, eels, and herring

Most of these fish live in the sea, but some eels and tarpon spend all, or at least part of their lives in fresh water. There are more than 730 species of eels, and they live in all oceans, except in polar areas. Eels have slender bodies and long fins on their backs and bellies. Tarpon belong to a small family of marine fish that are related to eels and herring. They have deeply forked tails. The herring group includes more than 350 species, some of which are important commercially as food. These include fish such as herring, sardines, and anchovies. Most are marine and live in schools in surface waters in the open sea or near coasts.

Alewife

Size: 15 in (38 cm)
Range: Atlantic coast of North America; northeastern Pacific Ocean
Scientific name: *Alosa pseudoharengus*

Alewife

A member of the herring group, the alewife feeds mostly on plankton and small fish. Although alewives live in the sea, they swim into rivers to mate and lay eggs, so they are often found in fresh water. The alewives that spend all their lives in lakes are only about half the size of sea-living alewives.

Tarpon

A strong, fast-swimming fish, the tarpon feeds on many types of fish and on crabs. The female lays millions of eggs in coastal waters, but many of the larvae drift into rivers, where they remain until they grow larger.

Tarpon

Size: 4–7¾ ft (1.2–2.4 m)
Range: Atlantic Ocean
Scientific name: *Tarpon atlanticus*

Atlantic herring

Herring have long been an important food for people, and large numbers of these fish are caught every year. In the sea they are also preyed on by birds, other fish, dolphins, and seals. Herring feed on plankton, small crustaceans, and fish.

Size: 15¾ in (40 cm)
Range: Atlantic and Pacific oceans
Scientific name: *Clupea harengus harengus*

Sardine

The sardine is similar to the herring but has a more rounded body and larger scales. Large schools of sardines swim in surface waters, feeding on animal plankton. Sardines are a valued food fish, and large numbers are caught by humans every year.

Sardine

Size: 9¾ in (25 cm)
Range: coasts of Europe
Scientific name: *Sardina pilchardus*

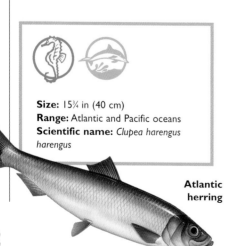

Atlantic herring

Snipe eel

This deep-sea eel has an extremely long, thin body, with fins that run almost its whole length. It has narrow, beaklike jaws and sharp, backward-facing teeth, which it uses to trap prey such as fish and crustaceans.

Snipe eel

Size: 3¼–4 ft (1–1.2 m)
Range: Atlantic, Pacific, and Indian oceans
Scientific name: *Nemichthys scolopaceus*

Spiny eel

The spiny eel has a long, slender body, but it is not a true eel. It has short spines on its back and belly. Little is known about this deep-sea fish, but it is thought to feed head down on the seafloor, eating bottom-living animals such as sea anemones.

Spiny eel

Size: 4 ft (1.2 m)
Range: North Atlantic Ocean
Scientific name: *Notacanthus chemnitzii*

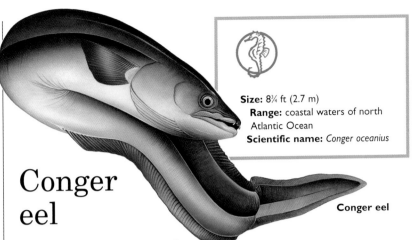

Size: 8¾ ft (2.7 m)
Range: coastal waters of north Atlantic Ocean
Scientific name: *Conger oceanius*

Conger eel

Conger eel

This eel is common on rocky north Atlantic shores. It usually lives in shallow water, where it hides among rocks and comes out to find fish, octopus, and other prey. Conger eels travel to deeper water to mate and lay their eggs. The eggs hatch into small transparent larvae that drift in the sea for a year or two before developing into small eels.

Mediterranean moray

Like all of the 100 or so different species of moray eels found in warm seas, this moray has a scaleless, boldly patterned body; powerful jaws; and strong, sharp teeth. A fierce hunter, the Mediterranean moray usually hides among rocks under water with only its head showing, watching out for prey such as fish, squid, and cuttlefish.

Mediterranean moray

Size: 4¼ ft (1.3 m)
Range: northeastern Atlantic Ocean, Mediterranean Sea
Scientific name: *Muraena helena*

European eel

Young eels live in fresh water, where they feed on insects, crustaceans, and fish. When they are ready to breed, they swim as far as 3,000 miles (4,800 km) out to sea, where they mate, lay eggs, and then die. The eggs hatch, and the larvae drift for about three years. They then swim into rivers, and the cycle starts all over again.

Size: 19¾ –39½ in (50–100 cm)
Range: north Atlantic Ocean
Scientific name: *Anguilla anguilla*

European eel

Salmon and stomiiformes

Hatchetfish

There are 76 different species of salmonidae, the family that includes salmon, trout, and char. They can be found in both fresh water and sea water, mainly in the northern hemisphere. Stomiiformes are usually deep-sea fish, with 320 species including hatchetfish and viperfish. They are some of the most common fish in the sea, and usually have large mouths, long teeth, and light organs which they use to attract prey in the dark, deep ocean.

Size: 2¾ in (7 cm)
Range: warm and tropical areas of all oceans
Scientific name: *Argyropelecus aculeatus*

Hatchetfish

This fish lives in water 1,300 to 2,000 feet (400 to 600 m) deep, but each night it comes up near the surface to find animal plankton to eat. On its belly are rows of light-producing organs, which give out a pale light. This confuses predators about the size and shape of the fish's body, making it harder to catch.

Sockeye salmon

Sockeye salmon

When they are about four years old, sockeye salmon move from the ocean to rivers. They swim to the same breeding grounds where they were hatched, sometimes as far as 1,000 miles (1,600 km) inland. After laying their eggs, the adult salmon die. The young spend up to three years in fresh water before migrating to the sea.

Size: 33 in (84 cm)
Range: Pacific Ocean
Scientific name: *Oncorhynchus nerka*

Rainbow trout

Now farmed in large quantities, rainbow trout are an important food fish. In the wild, rainbow trout live in rivers, although some spend part of their lives in the sea. In spring, the female makes a shallow nest in a stream and lays her eggs, which are then fertilized and covered over by the male.

Size: up to 3¼ ft (1 m)
Range: western North America; introduced worldwide
Scientific name: *Salmo gairdneri*

Atlantic salmon

Atlantic salmon

Like the sockeye, most Atlantic salmon swim into rivers to breed. The female makes a shallow nest on the riverbed in winter and lays her eggs, which are fertilized by the male. The eggs hatch the following spring, and the young spend two to six years in the river before going to sea.

Size: up to 5 ft (1.5 m)
Range: north Atlantic Ocean
Scientific name: *Salmo salar*

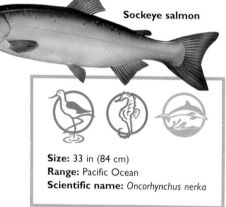

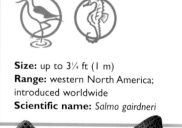

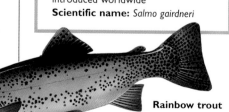
Rainbow trout

Powan

The powan is a member of the whitefish family, all of which have large scales, no teeth, and forked tails. Whitefish vary in size and appearance according to their habitat. Lake dwellers are generally much smaller than ocean dwellers because their food supply is often poor. Powan feed on planktonic crustaceans. They spawn in winter (ocean dwellers migrate into rivers to spawn).

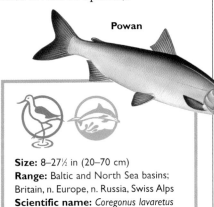

Powan

Size: 8–27½ in (20–70 cm)
Range: Baltic and North Sea basins; Britain, n. Europe, n. Russia, Swiss Alps
Scientific name: *Coregonus lavaretus*

Arctic char

Arctic char spend most of their lives in polar seas, feeding on fish and mollusks. When they are ready to breed, they swim into rivers, where females lay eggs among gravel on the riverbed. The young eventually make their way back to the sea. Some arctic char live in lakes.

Size: 9¾–37¾ in (25–96 cm)
Range: Arctic and north Atlantic oceans
Scientific name: *Salvelinus alpinus*

Trout

There are two forms of this well-known food fish: the sea trout, which migrates from river to sea and back to river to breed, and the smaller brown trout, which spends all its life in fresh water. They are alike physically, but sea trout have silvery scales with scattered black markings, and brown trout have numerous dark spots. Both types feed on fish and crustaceans.

Trout spawn in winter in gravel-bottomed fresh water, where the female makes a shallow nest for her eggs. The young hatch in spring and remain in the gravel for a few weeks.

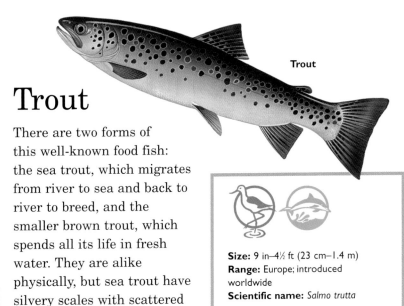

Trout

Size: 9 in–4½ ft (23 cm–1.4 m)
Range: Europe; introduced worldwide
Scientific name: *Salmo trutta*

Sloane's viperfish

Sloane's viperfish is one of six species of deep-sea viperfish. All viperfish have long, fanglike teeth. The skull is adapted to allow the jaws to open really wide to maximize the bite of the sharp teeth. The dorsal fin of the viperfish is positioned close behind the head; its first ray is very long and bears a light-producing organ to attract prey in the darkness of the deep sea. Viperfish feed on smaller fish, such as lanternfish. They follow their prey as they make their nightly migrations to waters nearer the surface in search of plankton to feed on.

Sloane's viperfish

Size: 11¾ in (30 cm)
Range: Atlantic, Pacific, and Indian oceans: temperate and tropical areas
Scientific name: *Chauliodus sloani*

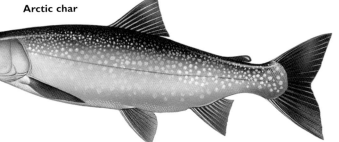

Arctic char

Cod and ophidiiformes

Ophidiiformes are mainly eel-like fish with long, tapering tails. There are 355 species, including the pearlfish and the New Zealand ling. They live in a wide range of habitats, such as sea caves and the deep ocean.

Cod are mainly marine fish (only five of the 480 species live in fresh water). The majority live in the northern hemisphere, from the shallow waters of the continental shelf to the deep ocean.

Size: 35½–39½ in (90–100 cm)
Range: north Atlantic Ocean
Scientific name: *Macrourus berglax*

Rough-head grenadier

A relative of the cod, the rough-head grenadier is a deep-sea fish with a large head and a tapering tail. Its body scales are rough and toothed. Males can make loud sounds by vibrating the swim bladder (a gas-filled sac inside the body) using special muscles.

Size: 5–6½ ft (1.5–2 m)
Range: northeastern Atlantic Ocean
Scientific name: *Molva molva*

Ling

The ling is most common in rocky-bottomed ocean waters, where it eats fish and large crustaceans. Although usually a deep-water fish, it may live in shallower areas where there are rocks. It breeds in spring and summer, and one female may lay as many as 60 million eggs.

Ling

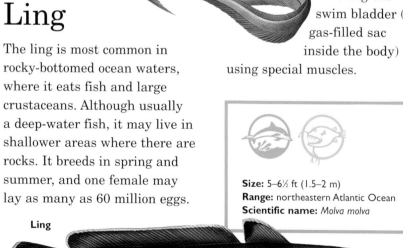

Atlantic cod

Cod usually swim in schools in surface waters but will search for food, such as other fish and worms, on the seafloor. Cod is an extremely valuable food fish for humans, but due to overfishing, fewer cod are caught each year.

Atlantic cod

Size: 4 ft (1.2 m)
Range: north Atlantic Ocean
Scientific name: *Gadus morhua*

Haddock

The haddock is a member of the cod family and feeds on bottom-living worms, mollusks, and brittle stars, as well as fish. It gathers in schools to spawn, and the eggs are left to float in the surface waters until they hatch. Young haddock often find shelter among the tentacles of large jellyfish.

Haddock

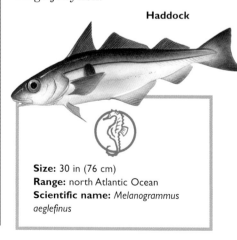

Size: 30 in (76 cm)
Range: north Atlantic Ocean
Scientific name: *Melanogrammus aeglefinus*

Walleye pollock

The pollock has a long, tapering body, three fins on its back, and two on its underside. Its head and mouth are large, and it has bigger eyes than most other kinds of cod. Unlike many cod, it feeds in midwaters, catching crustaceans and small fish.

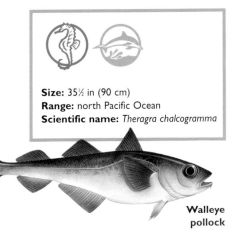

Size: 35½ in (90 cm)
Range: north Pacific Ocean
Scientific name: *Theragra chalcogramma*

Walleye pollock

Pearlfish

Pearlfish are small fish with spotted skin. Many spend much of their lives inside other animals, such as sea cucumbers and pearl oysters. Several pearlfish may live in one host. Young pearlfish pass through two larval stages before taking up residence in this way. In the first stage, the young fish float in surface waters; in the second, they live near the seabed. Adult pearlfish can live outside a host, feeding on crustaceans.

Size: 7¾ in (20 cm)
Range: Mediterranean and Adriatic seas
Scientific name: *Carapus acus*

Pearlfish

New Zealand ling

New Zealand ling

Not to be confused with the north Atlantic ling, this ling is one of a group known as cusk-eels, which belong to the cod order. A long, tapering fish, its dorsal, tail, and anal fins are joined to form one continuous strip around the body. Its head is flattened, and there are two thin pelvic fins under the lower jaw. The anus is positioned behind the head.

Size: 6–13¾ in (15–35 cm)
Range: European coasts: south Norway, British Isles to Mediterranean and Black seas
Scientific name: *Gaidropsarus mediterraneus*

White hake

The white hake has two dorsal fins, a rounded tail, and one long anal fin. It is found near soft, muddy seabeds, where it feeds. Spawning begins in late winter, and eggs and larvae float at the surface. Large quantities of white and red hake are fished commercially. These hakes are a separate group from the true hakes.

Size: 35½ in (90 cm)
Range: Seas off south Australia and New Zealand
Scientific name: *Genypterus blacodes*

Three-barbed rockling

The three-barbed is typical of most species of rockling, with its long, slender body and two dorsal fins. It also has three barbels—one on the chin and two on the snout. The rockling nearly always lives on rocky seabeds, and feeds on crustaceans, worms, and fish. It spawns offshore, and its eggs and larvae float on the surface. When the young are about 1½ inches (4 cm) long, they adopt the bottom-living habits of adult rocklings.

Three-barbed rockling

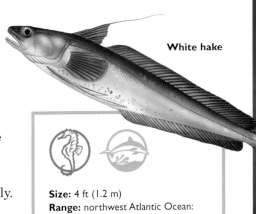

White hake

Size: 4 ft (1.2 m)
Range: northwest Atlantic Ocean: Gulf of St. Lawrence to Carolina
Scientific name: *Urophycis tenuis*

Anglerfish and toadfish

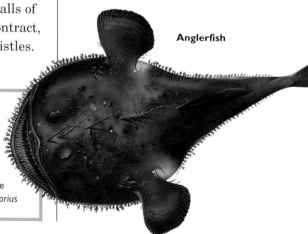

Atlantic football fish

Anglerfish are a distinctive family of fish with a flattened body dominated by a large, broad head. The head and mouth are fringed to hide the fish's shape. The first dorsal spine is long and used as a lure to attract prey. Anglerfish are bottom dwellers, living near the seafloor. Toadfish are so named because they look a little like toads, with a broad, flattened head, wide mouth, and bulging eyes.

Size: 23½ in (60 cm)
Range: all oceans
Scientific name: *Himantolophus groenlandicus*

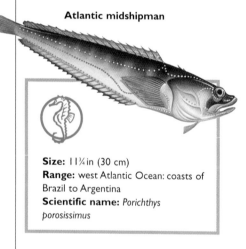

Atlantic midshipman

Size: 11¾ in (30 cm)
Range: west Atlantic Ocean: coasts of Brazil to Argentina
Scientific name: *Porichthys porosissimus*

Atlantic midshipman

The bottom-dwelling Atlantic midshipman has a large, flattened head with eyes near the top of the head. The body is scaleless, and has rows of light-producing organs on each side. They are among the few shallow-water fish to possess such organs. This species is also known as the singing fish because muscles in the walls of the fish's swim bladder contract, producing grunts and whistles.

Size: 3¼–6½ ft (1–2 m)
Range: coastal waters of Europe
Scientific name: *Lophius piscatorius*

Anglerfish

On its large head, the angler has a spine tipped with a flap of skin that it uses as a fishing lure. The fish lies on the seafloor and moves its lure to attract other fish. When something comes within reach, the angler opens its huge mouth and water flows in with the prey.

Atlantic football fish

This deep-sea anglerfish has a round body studded with bony plates, each with a central spine. On its head is a lure that carries a light-producing organ. It uses this lure to attract prey in the darkness of the deep sea.

Anglerfish

Linophryne

One of a family of deep-sea anglers, the linophryne has a rounded body and a branched chin barbel resembling a piece of seaweed. The strange "fishing rod" on its snout is branched and bears a glowing lure. The tiny adult males are believed to live parasitically on the females, losing their own powers of sight and smell.

Linophryne

Size: 2¾ in (7 cm)
Range: Atlantic, Pacific, Indian oceans
Scientific name: Linophryne arborifera

Longlure frogfish

The longlure frogfish has a plump body and a "fishing line" on its snout. Its variable coloration is designed to blend in with its surroundings, whether rock, coral, or seaweed. This slow-moving fish crawls around the seabed with the aid of its limblike pectoral fins, feeding on small fish and crustaceans.

Size: 6 in (15 cm)
Range: tropical west Atlantic Ocean and Caribbean Sea
Scientific name: Antennarius multiocellatus

Shortnose batfish

The shortnose batfish, with its almost triangular body, dramatically flattened from top to bottom, is typical of the 55 or so species of batfish. Its pectoral fins are large and flexible and positioned on armlike stalks. Its snout is pointed and its mouth small.

The upper surface of its body is studded with hard tubercles (rounded projections). A slow-moving, awkward swimmer, the batfish crawls over the seabed on its pectoral and pelvic fins, using its tail as support. It eats other fish, mollusks, crustaceans, and worms.

Size: 7½ in (19 cm)
Range: tropical areas of Atlantic, Indian, and Pacific oceans
Scientific name: Histrio histrio

Longlure frogfish

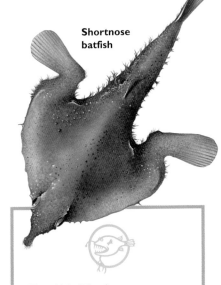

Shortnose batfish

Size: 11 in (28 cm)
Range: Caribbean Sea
Scientific name: Ogcocephalus nasutus

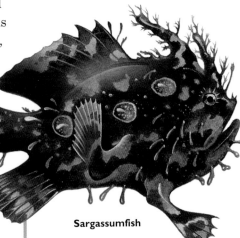

Sargassumfish

Sargassumfish

This is one of the family of anglers known as frogfishes. They have a balloon-shaped body covered with bumps and flaps of skin. Frondlike rays on its snout mimic the sargassum weed in which it lives. The sargassumfish attracts prey with the small lure on its snout. If it is attacked by a predator, it can take in water and pump itself into a ball too big to be swallowed.

Perchlike fish

This is the largest and most varied of all groups of fish, and species live in almost every watery habitat. This group is made up of at least 9,300 species—for example, sea bass, cichlids, gobies, and wrasses—with a wide range of body forms. Members include fish as different as the barracuda, angelfish, swordfish, and Siamese fightingfish. Despite their differences, all perchlike fish have one or two fins on their back, and most have pelvic fins close to the head. The pelvic fins usually have a spine and five rays.

Perch

Perch

Striped markings on the perch's body help camouflage it among water plants. It lives in slow-moving water and feeds on fish. Perch breed in shallow water in spring. The eggs are laid in long strings that wind around plants or other objects. They hatch in about eight days, and the young fish feed on plankton.

Size: 13¾–19¾ in (35–50 cm)
Range: Lakes and ponds of Europe
Scientific name: *Perca fluviatilis*

Size: 4 ft (1.2 m)
Range: Atlantic coastal waters, eastern Gulf of Mexico
Scientific name: *Mycteroperca bonaci*

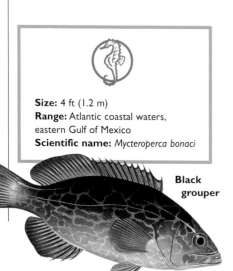

Black grouper

Black grouper

This common grouper can weigh up to 50 pounds (23 kg) when fully grown. It has a large head and irregular dark markings on the sides of its body. It is not a fast-moving fish and tends to lurk among rocks, waiting for prey to swim by. When something comes near, the grouper opens its large mouth and sucks the prey in with a mouthful of water. Young fish stay in shallow coastal areas, but adults move into deeper waters.

Orange-throat darter

This little member of the perch family feeds on insects and animal plankton. A breeding male has an orange throat and breast, whereas the female has a pale throat. The male chooses a nest site in a river and guards the eggs.

Orange-throat darter

Size: 3¼ in (8 cm)
Range: Rivers of the United States
Scientific name: *Etheostoma spectabile*

Greater amberjack

A relative of the pompano, the greater amberjack is a large fish with a sleek body and a deeply forked tail. It feeds on many species of fish and is caught as a game fish.

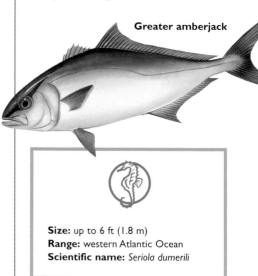

Greater amberjack

Size: up to 6 ft (1.8 m)
Range: western Atlantic Ocean
Scientific name: *Seriola dumerili*

Yellowtail snapper

Snappers are common around coral reefs and are a popular fish for people to eat. This species is easily recognized by its bright yellow tail and the yellow stripe along each side. It feeds mostly on other fish and small crustaceans.

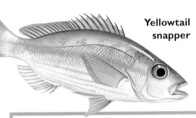

Yellowtail snapper

Size: 30 in (76 cm)
Range: western Atlantic Ocean, including Caribbean Sea
Scientific name: *Ocyurus chrysurus*

Bluefish

An extremely fierce hunter, the bluefish kills more prey than it can eat. It feeds on almost any fish, even the young of its own species. Schools of bluefish travel together, often following shoals of prey fish. Young bluefish, which are known as snappers, form their own separate schools.

Size: up to 4 ft (1.2 m)
Range: warm and tropical waters of Atlantic, Indian, and western Pacific oceans
Scientific name: *Pomatomus saltatrix*

Giant sea bass

This sea bass really is a giant. Some weigh more than 550 pounds (250 kg) and live for more than 70 years. They eat fish and crustaceans, and are themselves caught by humans for food. Young fish are redder in color and wider bodied than adults. They gradually develop their adult appearance by the time they are about 12 or 13 years old.

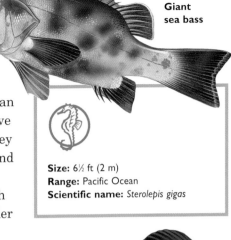

Giant sea bass

Size: 6½ ft (2 m)
Range: Pacific Ocean
Scientific name: *Sterolepis gigas*

Size: up to 5 ft (1.5 m)
Range: warm and tropical waters of all oceans
Scientific name:
Coryphaena hippurus

Florida pompano

The pompano has a rounded snout and a fairly wide body, which tapers sharply to a forked tail. It feeds mainly on mollusks and crustaceans, which it finds in the mud and sand of the seafloor. It is an excellent and valuable food fish.

Dolphinfish

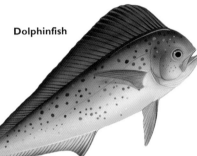

Dolphinfish

The brightly colored dolphinfish is easily identified by the large fin that runs along its back. The forehead of the male fish becomes steeper as he grows older; otherwise, males and females look alike. Dolphinfish move in small schools and eat fish, squid, and crustaceans. They are often seen around patches of floating seaweed, where their prey may hide.

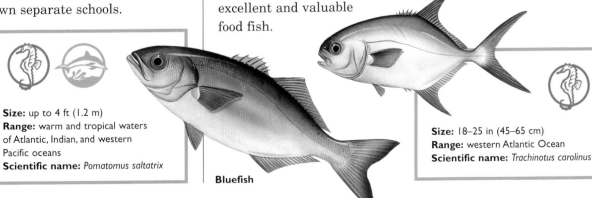

Florida pompano

Bluefish

Size: 18–25 in (45–65 cm)
Range: western Atlantic Ocean
Scientific name: *Trachinotus carolinus*

Blue tang

This fish has extremely sharp movable spines on each side of its tail that it can raise to wound an enemy. The young are bright yellow with blue markings. This color changes as the fish matures, becoming blue all over by the time it is an adult.

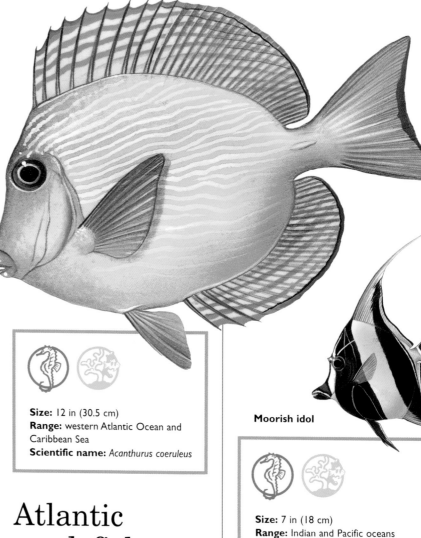

Young blue tang

Atlantic spadefish

Size: 12 in (30.5 cm)
Range: western Atlantic Ocean and Caribbean Sea
Scientific name: *Acanthurus coeruleus*

Size: 18–35 in (46–90 cm)
Range: western Atlantic Ocean
Scientific name: *Chaetodipterus faber*

Antarctic cod

This fish belongs to a group known as icefish. Many of them have a special substance in their blood that lowers its freezing point. As a result, icefish are able to survive at temperatures as low as 28.5°F (-1.9°C), at which most fish would freeze to death. This cod is a bottom dweller and eats mollusks, crustaceans, and worms, as well as some algae.

Atlantic spadefish

The coloration of this fish changes as it grows. Young fish are black, but they turn silvery gray with dark, vertical bars down the sides as they mature. The bars become less clear in large adults. Spadefish feed mostly on small invertebrates. They are often seen swimming around shipwrecks.

Size: 24 in (61 cm)
Range: coastal waters of Antarctica
Scientific name: *Notothenia coriiceps*

Moorish idol

Size: 7 in (18 cm)
Range: Indian and Pacific oceans
Scientific name: *Zanclus cornutus*

Moorish idol

This spectacular fish has bold stripes and a protruding snout. It has a wide body and long, swept-back fins. Although it is a relative of the blue tang, the moorish idol does not have tail spines. However, the young do have a sharp spine at each corner of their mouths. These spines drop off as the fish grow bigger.

Antarctic cod

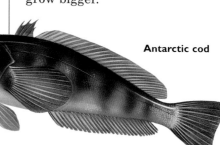

Redlip blenny

This fish is identified by the bristles on its rounded snout, its red lips, and its red-tipped dorsal fin. It lives on rocky or coral-bottomed seafloors, where it searches for small invertebrates to eat. The female lays her eggs among coral or under rocks, and the male guards them until they hatch.

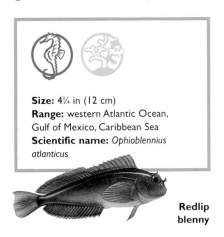

Size: 4¾ in (12 cm)
Range: western Atlantic Ocean, Gulf of Mexico, Caribbean Sea
Scientific name: *Ophioblennius atlanticus*

Redlip blenny

Rock goby

There are more than 1,800 kinds of gobies. Most live in the sea, but there are some freshwater species. The rock goby is one of the larger gobies but is typical of the group, with its big, blunt head and rounded tail. Its pelvic fins form a sucking disk, which it uses to cling to rocks. It feeds on small invertebrates and fish.

Rock goby

Size: 4¾ in (12 cm)
Range: north Atlantic Ocean and Mediterranean Sea
Scientific name: *Gobius paganellus*

Dragonet

The male dragonet, with his long blue-and-yellow fins, is a striking fish. The female is smaller and does not have extended fins. Dragonets lie half-buried in the sand on the seafloor, watching for bottom-dwelling crustaceans and worms—their main food. They breed in spring or summer, and males perform displays with their decorative fins to win females.

Northern stargazer

Size: up to 12 in (30.5 cm)
Range: Atlantic coast of North America
Scientific name: *Astroscopus guttatus*

Northern clingfish

The northern clingfish has a smooth body and a broad head. Its dorsal and anal fins are set back near its tail. Like all clingfish, its pelvic fins form part of a sucking disk on its belly. It uses this to cling to rocks or other surfaces, to keep from being washed away by strong tides in the coastal waters where it lives. Mollusks and crustaceans are the clingfish's main food.

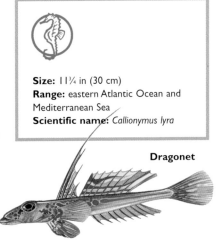

Size: 11¾ in (30 cm)
Range: eastern Atlantic Ocean and Mediterranean Sea
Scientific name: *Callionymus lyra*

Dragonet

Northern stargazer

The species has a large head with its mouth and eyes pointing upward. This allows the stargazer to lie buried on the seafloor, with only its eyes and mouth uncovered, watching for prey such as fish and crustaceans. Special organs behind the eyes produce electric charges to stun prey. Stargazers breed in deeper offshore waters, and the young drift into coastal waters, where they adjust to the bottom-dwelling life of adults.

Northern clingfish

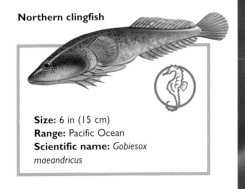

Size: 6 in (15 cm)
Range: Pacific Ocean
Scientific name: *Gobiesox maeandricus*

Tuna

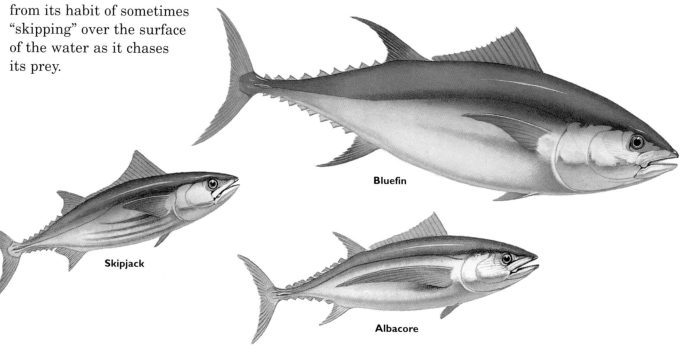

Bigeye

Species of tuna

The bluefin is the biggest of the tuna. It can grow to 10 feet (3 m) long and weigh more than 1,200 pounds (540 kg)—as much as seven or eight adult humans. A fast swimmer, the bluefin has been known to cross the Atlantic in 199 days.

The bigeye tuna grows to nearly 8 feet (2.4 m) long and can weigh more than 400 pounds (180 kg). The albacore and skipjack are smaller—up to 5 feet (1.5 m) and 3 feet (90 cm), respectively. The skipjack gets its name from its habit of sometimes "skipping" over the surface of the water as it chases its prey.

Among the fastest of all fish, tuna are shaped for speed and can swim at 50 miles per hour (80 km/h). They are the most streamlined of all fish, with pointed heads and torpedo-shaped bodies tapering to narrow tail stalks and crescent tails. The 13 species of tuna live in the surface waters of warm and tropical oceans. All are hunters, feeding mainly on fish and squid. Many swim in large schools, but the biggest fish swim in smaller groups or alone. Tuna rarely, if ever, stop swimming, because they must swim in order to breathe. Fish get their oxygen from water, not from air—their gills take oxygen out of the water as it flows over them. Most fish use muscles to pump water over their gills, but tuna are not able to do this. Instead they must keep swimming at all times to create a constant flow of water over their gills. The faster tuna swim, the more water passes over their gills, and the more oxygen they can extract from the water.

Skipjack

Bluefin

Albacore

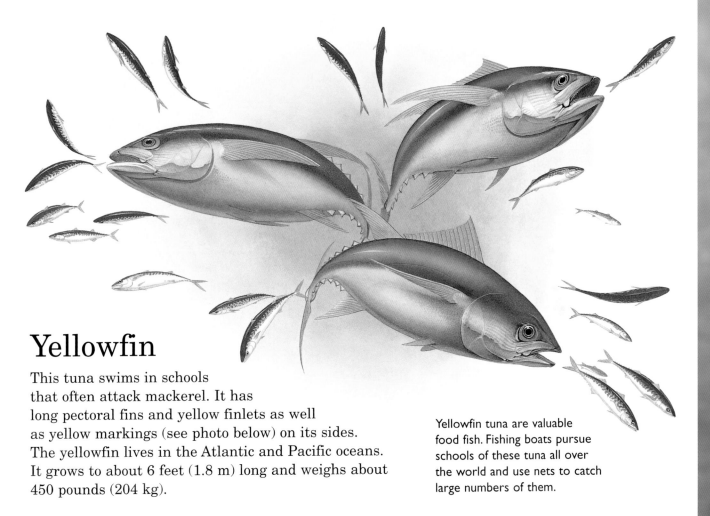

Yellowfin

This tuna swims in schools
that often attack mackerel. It has
long pectoral fins and yellow finlets as well
as yellow markings (see photo below) on its sides.
The yellowfin lives in the Atlantic and Pacific oceans.
It grows to about 6 feet (1.8 m) long and weighs about
450 pounds (204 kg).

Yellowfin tuna are valuable
food fish. Fishing boats pursue
schools of these tuna all over
the world and use nets to catch
large numbers of them.

Flyingfish, lanternfish, and lizardfish

Flyingfish belong to a large group of mostly sea-dwelling fish that also includes halfbeaks, needlefish, sauries, and garfish. Most are active near or above the surface of the water. Flyingfish can actually lift themselves into the air with their pectoral fins and use their rapidly beating tails to help them glide short distances over the surface. Lanternfish are deep-sea fish found in all oceans from the Arctic to the Antarctic. They have light-producing organs on their bodies. The lizardfish and its relative the bummalo both live in shallow coastal waters, where they prey on small fish.

Size: 17¾ in (45 cm)
Range: Atlantic Ocean
Scientific name: *Hemiramphus brasiliensis*

Ballyhoo

This fish cannot leap above the water like its relative the flyingfish, but it can skim over the surface. It moves in schools, feeding on sea grass and small fish, and may use its long lower jaw to scoop up food from the water's surface.

Lanternfish

This fish has groups of light-producing organs on its body. The arrangement of these is different in male and female fish. The light organs may help the fish to light up the dark depths of the sea to find prey, or they may be used to confuse the fish's enemies. Lanternfish feed on certain kinds of animal plankton.

Tropical two-wing flyingfish

Size: 9 in (23 cm)
Range: all oceans
Scientific name: *Exocetus volitans*

Tropical two-wing flyingfish

This flyingfish escapes its enemies by leaping up and gliding over the surface of the water with the aid of its winglike fins. Unlike some other species, this flyingfish has only one pair of "wings."

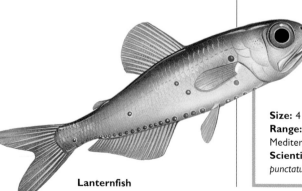

Lanternfish

Size: 4 in (10 cm)
Range: north Atlantic Ocean, Mediterranean Sea
Scientific name: *Myctophum punctatum*

Red lizardfish

Size: 12½ in (32 cm)
Range: Atlantic Ocean
Scientific name: *Synodus synodus*

Red lizardfish

The red lizardfish has long pelvic fins and often lies on the seafloor, supporting its body on these fins. A fierce hunter, it lies in wait for prey, and then suddenly darts up from the sea bottom and catches its target in its long, sharp teeth.

Garfish

Size: 37 in (94 cm)
Range: north Atlantic Ocean, Mediterranean and Black seas
Scientific name: *Belone belone*

Garfish

The slender garfish can live for up to 18 years. An active hunter, it eats small fish and crustaceans. Garfish breed in coastal waters, and the small, round eggs attach themselves to floating debris or seaweed.

Bummalo

Atlantic saury

Sauries swim in schools in surface waters, feeding on small fish and crustaceans. They have beaklike jaws, the lower longer than the upper. The young hatch with short jaws of equal length; the long lower jaw develops as the hatchlings grow.

Size: 16¼ in (41 cm)
Range: Indian Ocean
Scientific name: *Harpadon nehereus*

Bummalo

The bummalo has a long body and huge jaws armed with sharp, curving teeth. It is often found near the mouths of large rivers, where it eats small fish and crustaceans. This fish is split and dried in the sun for eating. In this form it is known as Bombay duck!

Size: 15¾–19¾ in (40–50 cm)
Range: north Atlantic Ocean and Mediterranean Sea
Scientific name: *Scomberesox saurus*

Atlantic saury

Guppies, grunions, and relatives

Guppies belong to a large group of fish that contains more than 800 species, including four-eyed fish. Most are surface swimmers and feed on insects and plant matter that has fallen into the water. They are extremely adaptable and able to survive in stagnant, slow-moving water that is unsuitable for most other fish.

Grunions belong to a group of more than 280 species that includes silversides, sand smelt, and rainbow fish. Most feed on animal plankton and live in large schools in lakes, estuaries, and shallow coastal waters.

Sand smelt

Sand smelt

This small fish swims in schools. It has a long, slender body and two widely spaced fins on its back. Animal plankton is its main food, but it also eats tiny fish. The sand smelt is in turn eaten by larger fish and by seabirds such as terns.

Size: 6–8 in (15–20 cm)
Range: eastern Atlantic Ocean
Scientific name: *Atherina presbyter*

California grunion

Grunions time their breeding with the rhythms of the tides. On the night of an extremely high tide, they swim ashore and lay their eggs in the sand. The next wave carries the fish back to the sea. Two weeks later, at the next high tide, the eggs hatch and the young are carried out to sea.

California grunion

Size: 7 in (18 cm)
Range: Pacific Ocean
Scientific name: *Leuresthes tenuis*

Hardhead silverside

During the day, the slender body of this little fish looks almost transparent, with a narrow silvery stripe running down each side, but when night falls its color darkens. Silversides are common fish, and they swim together in large schools. Their eggs have tiny threads that attach them to water plants while the embryos are developing.

Hardhead silverside

Size: 5 in (12.5 cm)
Range: north Atlantic Ocean
Scientific name: *Atherinomorus stipes*

Four-eyed fish

Size: 11¾ in (30 cm)
Range: coasts and lakes of Central America and northern South America
Scientific name: *Anableps anableps*

Four-eyed fish

This unusual fish has only two eyes, but they are divided into two parts. The top part of each eye is for seeing in the air, and the lower part is for seeing under water. The two parts are separated by a dark band. The fish swims at the surface, with the water reaching the dividing bands on the eyes. It is able to watch for insects in the air and prey in the water at the same time.

Size: 4–6 in (10–15 cm)
Range: coasts of North America
Scientific name: *Fundulus heteroclitus*

Mummichog

The stout-bodied mummichog is a hardy little fish that can survive in salt or fresh water and eats almost any plant or animal it can find. It breeds in the spring in shallow water. The male chases his mate and then clasps her with his fins so that he can fertilize the eggs as they are laid. The eggs stick together and sink to the bottom in a cluster.

Size: 3 in (7.5 cm)
Range: Atlantic coast of U.S.A.: Cape Cod, south to Mexico
Scientific name: *Cyprinidon variegatus*

Sheepshead minnow

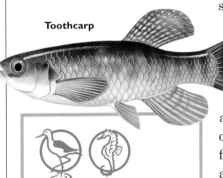

Mummichog

Toothcarp

Size: 3¼ in (8 cm)
Range: Indian Ocean: coasts of east Africa and Middle East; Red Sea
Scientific name: *Aphanius dispar*

Sheepshead minnow

Except for the breeding season, when males develop brighter coloration, male and female sheepshead minnows look similar. The female lays her eggs a few at a time while the male fertilizes them. The eggs have sticky threads on the surface that bind the eggs to each other and to plants.

Toothcarp

The toothcarp is found in fresh- and saltwater pools and in the sea. Males and females of the species differ in color. Males are brownish blue with dark markings near and on the tail, while females are grayish blue with markings on their sides. The toothcarp feeds on small invertebrates and algae. The female deposits her eggs on submerged aquatic plants. The eggs hatch in under two weeks, and the young feed on plant plankton and algae.

Squirrelfish, oarfish, and relatives

Opah

All of these fish live in the sea. Squirrelfish, pinecone fish, roughie, and beardfish all belong to a group of about 123 species of wide, or deep-bodied, fish with spiny fins. The oarfish and opah belong to a rare group about which little is known. The John Dory belongs to a separate group of deep-bodied fish, many of which live in deep water. The whalefish is a deep-sea species.

Size: 6 ft (1.5 m)
Range: worldwide except Antarctica
Scientific name: *Lampris guttatus*

Opah

Despite its almost comical appearance, this fish is a successful hunter, feeding on squid and fish such as hake and whiting. It has a large, rounded body dotted with white spots, and bright red fins. It may weigh as much as 600 pounds (270 kg).

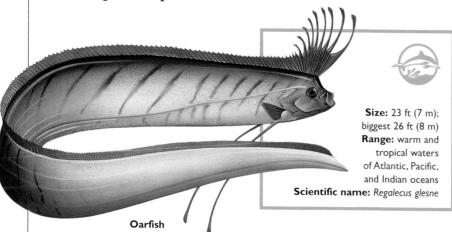

Oarfish

Size: 23 ft (7 m); biggest 26 ft (8 m)
Range: warm and tropical waters of Atlantic, Pacific, and Indian oceans
Scientific name: *Regalecus glesne*

Oarfish

This unusual fish has a long ribbonlike body with a dorsal fin running along most of its length. It swims with rippling snakelike movements and is thought to have been the source of many tales about giant sea serpents. The oarfish has no teeth in its small mouth and feeds mainly on small shrimplike crustaceans.

Squirrelfish

This brightly colored fish is commonly found on coral reefs. After spending the day hiding in crevices in the reef, it comes out at night to hunt for small crustaceans and other prey. Its large eyes help it see well in the darkness. A squirrelfish can make a range of sounds by using special muscles to vibrate its swim bladder (a gas-filled sac inside the body).

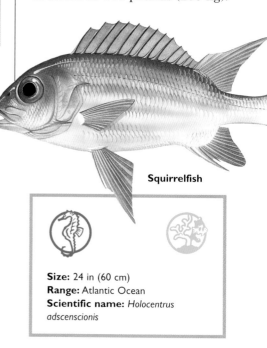

Squirrelfish

Size: 24 in (60 cm)
Range: Atlantic Ocean
Scientific name: *Holocentrus adscenscionis*

Pinecone fish

The body of the pinecone fish is protected by an armor of heavy platelike scales. Its dorsal fin consists of thick spines, and it has more spines on its underside. Under the lower jaw it has two light-producing organs. Pinecone fish move in schools near the bottom of the sea.

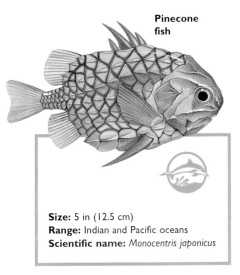

Pinecone fish

Size: 5 in (12.5 cm)
Range: Indian and Pacific oceans
Scientific name: *Monocentris japonicus*

Whalefish

This is a small fish with a big name. It has a large head for its size and no scales on its body. The area at the base of the dorsal and anal fins is thought to glow in the dark. It hunts for its food and seizes prey in its large jaws, which are lined with many tiny teeth.

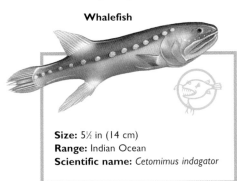

Whalefish

Size: 5½ in (14 cm)
Range: Indian Ocean
Scientific name: *Cetomimus indagator*

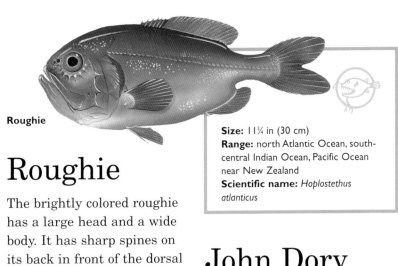

Roughie

Size: 11¾ in (30 cm)
Range: north Atlantic Ocean, south-central Indian Ocean, Pacific Ocean near New Zealand
Scientific name: *Hoplostethus atlanticus*

Roughie

The brightly colored roughie has a large head and a wide body. It has sharp spines on its back in front of the dorsal fin and on its belly in front of the anal fin. Its large mouth points up, and its jaws are lined with lots of tiny teeth. Little is known about the habits of this fish, but it is thought to feed on small crustaceans.

John Dory

Size: 16–26 in (40–66 cm)
Range: eastern Atlantic Ocean, Mediterranean Sea
Scientific name: *Zeus faber*

John Dory

The John Dory has 9 or 10 thick spines in the front part of its dorsal fin and 3 or 4 spines in the front part of its anal fin. This fish is not a fast swimmer and catches its food by stealth, not speed. It approaches its prey, such as small fish and crustaceans, slowly, until near enough to snap them up in its huge mouth. The John Dory is a popular food fish in Europe.

Stout beardfish

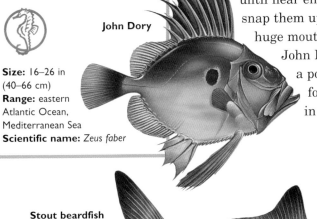

Stout beardfish

This fish takes its name from the pair of whiskers, or barbels, that hang from its lower jaw. These may help it find food on the seafloor. It usually lives at depths of about 600 to 2,100 feet (180 to 640 m).

Size: 9¾ in (25 cm)
Range: tropical areas of all oceans
Scientific name: *Polymixia nobilis*

Gasterosteiform fish

Gasterosteiformes do not have scales but are armored with bony plates. There are about 260 species in the order, including sticklebacks, seahorses, and pipefish. The sticklebacks and their relatives, the tubesnouts, are spiny-finned fish that live both in the sea and in fresh water. The strangely shaped seahorses and pipefish live in shallow seawater. They cannot move fast and rely on camouflage to hide them from predators.

Threespine stickleback

In the breeding season, the male threespine stickleback develops a red belly. He builds a nest from bits of plants glued together with mucus. He then displays his belly to attract females to his nest to lay their eggs. He fertilizes the eggs and guards them carefully until they hatch about three weeks later.

Threespine stickleback

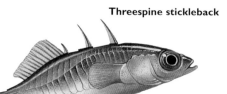

Size: 2–4 in (5–10 cm)
Range: coasts and fresh water of North America, Europe, and northern Asia
Scientific name: *Gasterosteus aculeatus*

Fourspine stickleback

This stickleback prefers areas with plenty of seaweed. Its body is bare, lacking the bony plates of the threespine stickleback. Small crustaceans are its main food.

Fourspine stickleback

Size: 2¼ in (6 cm)
Range: coasts and fresh water of eastern North America
Scientific name: *Apeltes quadracus*

Fifteenspine stickleback

This stickleback has a long body and a pointed snout. It has between 14 and 17 (usually 15) spines on its back. It lives in the sea and feeds on small crustaceans.

Fifteenspine stickleback

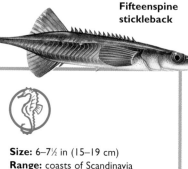

Size: 6–7½ in (15–19 cm)
Range: coasts of Scandinavia and northern Europe
Scientific name: *Spinachia spinachia*

Tubesnout

The tubesnout has a long body and a small mouth at the tip of its extended snout. It has 24 to 26 spines along its back. Tubesnouts move in large schools of hundreds, or even thousands, of individual fish. They feed on small crustaceans and other plankton.

Size: 6¼ in (16 cm)
Range: western coast of North America
Scientific name: *Aulorhynchus flavidus*

Tubesnout

Winged dragon

A strange fish, the winged dragon has a broad, flattened body, surrounded with bony rings, and a tapering tail. Its snout is long and also flattened with a small mouth on the underside. Its pectoral fins are broad and winglike, while its other fins are relatively small.

Winged dragon

Size: 5½ in (14 cm)
Range: coastal waters of the Indian and Pacific oceans, from East Africa to northern Australia
Scientific name: *Pegasus volitans*

Shrimpfish

The shrimpfish often swims in a vertical position with its long snout held downward. It pushes itself through the water using its tail and anal fins. It is often found among the spines of sea urchins, where dark stripes along the sides of its body mimic the urchins' spines and provide camouflage.

Shrimpfish

Size: 6 in (15 cm)
Range: Indian and Pacific oceans from east Africa to northern Australia
Scientific name: *Aeoliscus strigatus*

Greater pipefish

The body of the greater pipefish is covered in bony armor. The male pipefish incubates the eggs in a pouch of skin located under its tail. The eggs are incubated for about five weeks, after which the perfectly formed young are released through a slit in the pouch.

Size: 12–18 in (30–47 cm)
Range: coastal waters of the eastern Atlantic Ocean and the Mediterranean and Adriatic seas
Scientific name: *Syngnathus acus*

Weedy sea dragon

Sea dragons are closely related to seahorses. Sea dragons have leaflike flaps of skin on their bodies that are thought to help them hide from enemies among fronds of seaweed. The male incubates his mate's eggs on a flap of skin beneath his tail.

Weedy sea dragon

Size: 18 in (47 cm)
Range: coastal waters of southern Australia
Scientific name: *Phyllopteryx taeniolatus*

Dwarf seahorse

This unusual fish moves slowly, gently pushing itself along with the movements of its tiny dorsal fin. It can also attach itself to seaweed by curling its tail around it. In the breeding season the female lays 50 or more eggs, which she places in a pouch on the male's body, where they incubate and then hatch.

Dwarf seahorse

Size: 1½ in (4 cm)
Range: coastal waters of the Gulf of Mexico and Caribbean Sea
Scientific name: *Hippocampus zosterae*

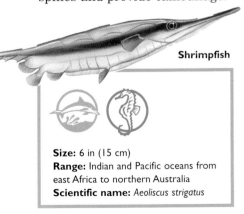

Zones of the sea

Scientists divide the underwater world of the oceans into different depth zones. These zones differ in their physical conditions, such as light level, temperature, and water pressure. Each zone supports a community of organisms specially adapted to that environment. The presence or absence of light determines the nature and numbers of ocean creatures. In the clearest oceans, sunlight only penetrates to a depth of 3,000 feet (900 m), and most is absorbed in the first 650 feet (200 m). Water temperature drops with depth, and in the very deep ocean, water pressure is 1,000 times greater than at the surface.

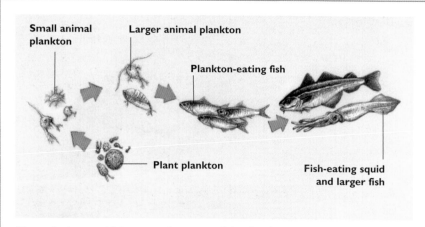

Plant plankton, which are at the start of the food chain, are consumed by animal plankton. These are eaten by larger animal plankton and small fish. Top predators include larger fish.

Sea food chain

Ocean creatures depend on plants, directly or indirectly, for their survival. Tiny plants called phytoplankton trap sunlight to make their own food. They are eaten by small animal plankton (zooplankton) which, in turn, are eaten by larger zooplankton. Small fish strain seawater with their gills to extract plankton. Larger predators feed on the smaller fish. Deep-sea creatures feed on the remains of dead plants and animals that fall to the ocean floor.

The sunlit zone
This zone extends to a depth of 650 feet (200 m). Here there is enough sunlight to fuel the growth of green plants. Drifting microscopic algae, or phytoplankton, are numerous and are eaten by many other organisms. The plants of the sunlit zone—directly or indirectly—provide the food for almost all the animals of the open ocean.

The twilight zone
Dim sunlight penetrates to this level, but not enough to sustain the growth of plants. In the strange half-light, many fish and squid generate their own light (bioluminescence). Their dark and light skin patterns break up their outline, making them less visible to predators. Many inhabitants of the twilight zone rise to the surface waters at night to feed on phytoplankton.

The dark zone
In the cold, dark waters of this zone there is no sunlight at all. The creatures that inhabit the dark zone are often scary—with huge mouths and small bodies—but on a miniature scale. Most of the fish are much less than 3 feet (0.9 m) long. There is little food at this depth, and fish cannot afford to let any prey escape, so they generally have big jaws and long, sharp teeth.

The abyss
This high-pressure environment is colder than the dark zone, and food is even more scarce. Animals gather on or just above the seafloor, and feed on waste matter or dead animals that drift down. The community of fish, crabs, shrimp, and amphipods can strip a carcass to the bone within hours.

The viperfish uses its razor-sharp teeth and large, gaping jaw to catch its prey.

KEY

1 Portuguese man-of-war	14 Squid
2 Reef shark	15 Cod
3 Green turtle	16 Lanternfish
4 Flying fish	17 Giant squid
5 Bluefin tuna	18 Hatchetfish
6 Plankton	19 Dragonfish
7 Dolphin	20 Anglerfish
8 Seaweed	21 Gulper eel
9 Mackerel	22 Viperfish
10 Blue whale	23 Stalked sea lillies
11 Sperm whale	24 Tripod fish
12 Shrimp	25 Sea cucumber
13 Manta ray	26 Brittle stars

Scorpionfish

This large, widely distributed order contains 24 families and nearly 1,300 species of fish, most of which live in the sea. Their body shape varies, but most species are thick-set and spiny. Some species in this group, such as the stonefish, protect themselves by producing powerful poisons. These can prove fatal to humans who accidentally step on a fish.

Bullrout

Also known as the shorthorn sculpin, this fish has spines near its gills and along each side. Females are usually larger than males. A bottom dweller, the bullrout eats seafloor crustaceans as well as worms and small fish.

Bullrout

Size: 10–23½ in (25–60 cm)
Range: north Atlantic Ocean
Scientific name: *Myoxocephalus scorpius*

Lionfish

Lionfish

With its brightly striped body and large fanlike fins, this fish is one of the most extraordinary in the sea. The spines on its back are poisonous and can be dangerous even for humans. The fish uses its spines to defend itself against enemies, not to attack prey.

Size: 15 in (38 cm)
Range: Indian and Pacific oceans
Scientific name: *Pterois volitans*

Northern sea robin

A relative of the lionfish, the northern sea robin spends much of its life on the seafloor, often supporting itself on its pectoral fins. It uses the first three spines of its pectoral fins to feel for prey on the seafloor. When it is in danger, the sea robin buries itself in sand, leaving only the top of its head and eyes showing.

Stonefish

The stonefish's mottled coloring and irregular shape keep it well hidden as it lies half-buried among stones on the seafloor. The sharp spines on its back are linked to glands containing a deadly poison that can kill a person unlucky enough to step on a stonefish's spines.

Stonefish

Size: 11¾ in (30 cm)
Range: Indian and Pacific Oceans
Scientific name: *Synanceia verrucosa*

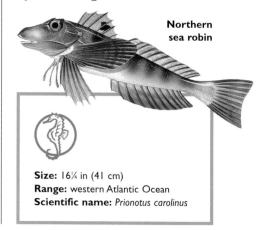

Northern sea robin

Size: 16¼ in (41 cm)
Range: western Atlantic Ocean
Scientific name: *Prionotus carolinus*

Rascasse

The rascasse lurks amid seaweed-covered rocks, where its camouflage coloring and the weedlike flaps of skin on its head make it almost invisible. Its dorsal fin is spiny, with venom glands at the sides of the spines. The fish breed in spring or early summer. Eggs are shed in a mass of sticky mucus.

Rascasse

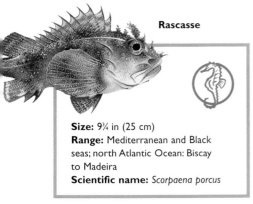

Size: 9¾ in (25 cm)
Range: Mediterranean and Black seas; north Atlantic Ocean: Biscay to Madeira
Scientific name: *Scorpaena porcus*

Redfish

A heavy-bodied fish, with a large head and a jutting lower jaw, the redfish has a strongly spined dorsal fin and three spines on the anal fin. By day it stays close to the bottom, but at night it rises to the surface to feed on fish such as herring and cod. Redfish give birth to live young.

Size: 32–39 in (80–100 cm)
Range: north Atlantic Ocean: Arctic to Scotland and northern U.S.A.
Scientific name: *Sebastes marinus*

Redfish

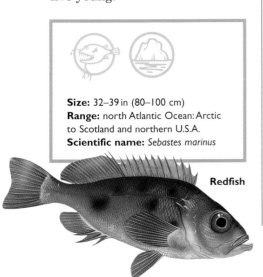

Kelp greenling

The kelp greenling is one of 11 species of greenling, all found in the north Pacific Ocean. Its head is smooth with no spines or ridges, and it has large pectoral fins and a long dorsal fin with a notch halfway along its length. Kelp greenlings eat worms, crustaceans, and small fish, and are in turn preyed on by larger fish and birds.

Size: up to 11¾ in (30 cm)
Range: north Pacific Ocean: North American coast, Bering Sea to California
Scientific name: *Agonus acipenserinus*

Sturgeon poacher

Lumpsucker

The lumpsucker has a round body studded with rows of spined plates along the sides. Its skin is scaleless. Its ventral fins form a powerful suction disk on its belly with which the lumpsucker attaches itself to the seabed, or to rocks and other debris. It feeds on small crustaceans, jellyfish, and other invertebrates, as well as some small fish. Females are larger than males.

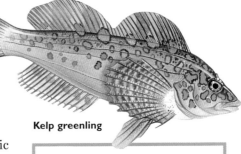

Kelp greenling

Size: 20¾ in (53 cm)
Range: Pacific Ocean coast of North America: Alaska to California
Scientific name: *Hexagrammos decagrammus*

Sturgeon poacher

A long, very slender fish, the sturgeon poacher has a body armor of bony plates. It has several spines on its large sturgeonlike head, and clusters of slender barbels around its mouth. It lives near or on the seabed and feeds mainly on crustaceans and marine worms. Although common, unlike the sturgeon it is not caught as a food fish.

Lumpsucker

Size: 11¾–23½ in (30–60 cm)
Range: north Atlantic Ocean: Arctic to Scandinavia, Iceland, British Isles, Newfoundland to New Jersey
Scientific name: *Cyclopterus lumpus*

Flatfish

The flatfish belong to a group of about 570 species. All but three of these live in the sea. Young flatfish have rounded bodies at first, but as they grow their bodies flatten and the eye on one side moves so that both eyes are on the upper surface. A typical flatfish spends much of its life on the seafloor, lying with its eyes facing up. Some flatfish have both eyes on the right side; others have them on the left.

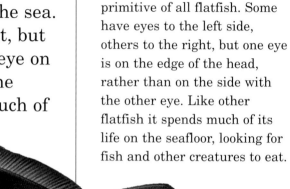

Adalah

Adalah

The adalah is the most primitive of all flatfish. Some have eyes to the left side, others to the right, but one eye is on the edge of the head, rather than on the side with the other eye. Like other flatfish it spends much of its life on the seafloor, looking for fish and other creatures to eat.

Size: up to 24 in (61 cm)
Range: Red Sea, Indian Ocean, western Pacific Ocean
Scientific name: *Psettodes erumei*

California halibut

This halibut has a large mouth and strong, sharp teeth. It feeds on fish, particularly anchovies, and is itself eaten by creatures such as rays, sea lions, and porpoises. It is also an important food fish for people. A large halibut of this species can weigh up to 70 pounds (32 kg).

California halibut

Size: 5 ft (1.5 m)
Range: Pacific Ocean
Scientific name: *Paralichthys californicus*

Turbot

This broad-bodied flatfish varies in color, but it usually has speckled markings that help keep it hidden as it lies on the seafloor. Adult turbots feed mostly on fish, but young turbots eat small crustaceans. Turbots breed in spring or summer, and females produce as many as ten million eggs.

Turbot

Size: 3¼ ft (1 m)
Range: eastern Atlantic Ocean, Mediterranean Sea
Scientific name: *Scopthalmus maximus*

Summer flounder

Size: up to 3¼ ft (1 m)
Range: western Atlantic Ocean
Scientific name: *Paralichthys dentatus*

Summer flounder

A slender, active fish, the summer flounder feeds on crustaceans, mollusks, and fish, and will chase prey into surface waters if necessary. But although a fast swimmer, it spends much of its life lying half-buried on the seafloor. Its color varies according to the type of sea bottom it is on so that it can be camouflaged.

Plaice

The top side of this flatfish is brown with orange spots. Plaice larvae live in surface waters for up to six weeks before starting a bottom-dwelling life.

Plaice

Size: 19¾–36 in (50–91 cm)
Range: eastern Atlantic Ocean, Mediterranean Sea
Scientific name: *Pleuronectes platessa*

Sole

Normally a nighttime feeder, the sole usually spends the day buried in sand or mud. It breeds in shallow water, and the eggs float at the surface until they hatch. Larvae live at the surface but move to the seafloor when they are about a half-inch (1.25 cm) long.

Sole

Size: 11¾–23½ in (30–60 cm)
Range: eastern Atlantic Ocean, Mediterranean Sea
Scientific name: *Solea solea*

Size: 7¾ in (20 cm)
Range: western Atlantic Ocean
Scientific name: *Symphurus plagusia*

Naked sole

Size: up to 9 in (23 cm)
Range: northwestern Atlantic Ocean
Scientific name: *Gymnachirus melas*

Naked sole

The naked sole has no scales on its skin and is marked with dark stripes on its upper side. The underside is whiteish in color. Most of these fish have both eyes on the right side, and the mouth is also twisted to the right.

The naked sole spends most of its life on the seafloor, but it is an active hunter and can swim well when necessary.

Blackcheek tonguefish

This flatfish has a body that is broad at the front and tapers to a pointed tail. Both of its eyes are on the left side of the head, and its mouth is also twisted to the left. It lives on the seafloor and feeds on invertebrate animals such as crustaceans.

Blackcheek tonguefish

Coelacanth and triggerfish

The coelacanth is thought to resemble some of the earliest fish. Common millions of years ago, only one species now survives. Its limblike fins allow it to "walk" along the ocean floor. Triggerfish and their relatives, the pufferfish and boxfish, belong to a group of about 340 species, many of which have round or boxlike bodies.

Porcupinefish

The body of this fish is covered with long, sharp spines that normally lie flat. But if it is in danger, it puffs up its body so the spines stand out, making it almost impossible for any predator to catch. It has two teeth in each jaw. These teeth are joined together to make a sharp beak for crushing hard-shelled prey such as mollusks and crabs.

Porcupinefish

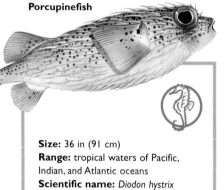

Size: 36 in (91 cm)
Range: tropical waters of Pacific, Indian, and Atlantic oceans
Scientific name: *Diodon hystrix*

Size: 22 in (56 cm)
Range: western Atlantic Ocean and Caribbean Sea
Scientific name: *Balistes vetula*

Queen triggerfish

Queen triggerfish

The triggerfish has three spines on its back. When the first spine is upright, it is locked into place by the second. When in danger, the triggerfish can wedge itself into a crevice with this "locking" spine and make itself extremely hard to move. It feeds on small invertebrate creatures, particularly sea urchins.

Scrawled filefish

A relative of the triggerfish, this filefish has a long spine on its back and small prickly spines on the scales of its body. It lives on bottom-living invertebrates and seaweeds. It often lurks in clumps of eelgrass, where its coloration keeps it well hidden.

Scrawled filefish

Size: 36 in (91 cm)
Range: tropical waters of Atlantic, Pacific, and Indian oceans
Scientific name: *Aluterus scriptus*

Blue-spotted boxfish

Like all boxfish, this fish has a hard shell around its body, made up of joined plates. Its mouth, eyes, fins, and gill openings are the only breaks in the armor, which protects the fish from its enemies. It feeds mostly on bottom-living invertebrate creatures.

Blue-spotted boxfish

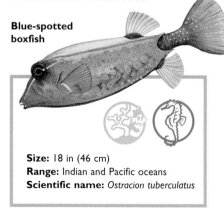

Size: 18 in (46 cm)
Range: Indian and Pacific oceans
Scientific name: *Ostracion tuberculatus*

Coelacanth

Coelacanths were thought to have been extinct for millions of years until one was caught off the coast of South Africa in 1938. This living species is still very much like its fossil relatives. It has a heavy body and fleshy sections at the base of all its fins except the first dorsal fin. It is believed to hunt other fish to eat.

Coelacanth

Size: 6½ ft (2 m)
Range: Indian Ocean
Scientific name: *Latimeria chalumnae*

Size: 13 in (33 cm)
Range: Indian and Pacific oceans: east Africa to India, Southeast Asia, Australia, and Japan
Scientific name: *Balistoides conspicillum*

Clown triggerfish

The clown triggerfish has large, light spots on the lower half of its body, green markings on its back and tail fin, and its mouth is circled with bright orange. Its second dorsal and anal fins are smaller than many triggerfish, but, like all members of the family Balistidae, the first dorsal spine can be locked into an erect position by the second.

Ocean sunfish

The ocean sunfish is a relative of the triggerfish, but it is quite unlike any other fish. Its body is almost completely round and ends in a curious frill-like tail. Despite its huge size, it has a small beaklike mouth and feeds on creatures such as animal plankton and tiny jellyfish.

Clown triggerfish

Pufferfish

A member of the family Tetraodontidae, the pufferfish's body is stout behind the head and tapers toward a forked tail. The skin on its back is smooth, but when it inflates its body with water, small spines embedded in its belly stand erect as a defensive device. Like all pufferfish, it also has beaklike jaws, formed by one pair of partially fused teeth in each jaw. It is believed to feed on fish, crustaceans, and squid.

Size: up to 13 ft (4 m)
Range: Atlantic, Pacific, and Indian oceans
Scientific name: *Mola mola*

Ocean sunfish

Pufferfish

Size: 24 in (61 cm)
Range: tropical and subtropical Atlantic Ocean, occasionally as far north as Britain; Indian and Pacific oceans
Scientific name: *Lagocephalus lagocephalus*

Coral

Coral reefs contain the richest variety of life in the world's oceans. The reefs are made up of the skeletons of thousands of coral animals called polyps—relatives of the sea anemone. During their lives, polyps make hard skeletons around themselves. A living polyp has a simple, cuplike body with a single opening surrounded by tentacles, which are armed with stinging cells. The polyp uses these tentacles to catch food, which is then passed to the mouth in the center of its body. Polyps can only live in warm water 70°F (21°C) or above. A coral reef is also home to a variety of other animals. Small fish, mollusks, and crustaceans feed on marine plants living on the coral, as well as on the coral itself.

Fringing coral reefs surround the islands of Palau.

A strange partnership

Coral reefs may grow many miles long, but they are created by tiny organisms, most of which are less than 0.3 inches (1 cm) across. Each polyp creates a hard protective skeleton of limestone around itself. It also harbors welcome guests called zooxanthellae— special algae that live within its body. The algae trap sunlight and manufacture food for the polyp. In return, the polyp provides a safe home.

How coral reefs form

When coral polyps die, their chalky skeletons remain behind. New polyps settle on top, so the reef grows. The polyps only grow in warm, sun-drenched seawater. Under these conditions, fringing reefs form in shallow water along coasts. If the nearby land sinks, the reef continues to grow offshore, forming a barrier reef. When a fringing reef develops around a volcanic island and the island sinks, a circular barrier reef forms. If the island then sinks completely, a coral atoll—a ring of coral—remains.

Fringing reef   Barrier reef   Coral atoll

The diagram shows how the three main types of coral reefs form.

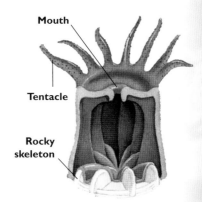

Mouth

Tentacle

Rocky skeleton

It takes thousands of these coral polyps to make a clump of coral.

A pink anemonefish is immune to the stinging tentacles of its host anemone.

Every nook and cranny

There are hundreds of different kinds of coral. Coral grows in many colors and shapes resembling ferns, deer antlers, mushrooms, and even human brains, and creates an intricate patchwork in the sea where plants and animals can settle or hide. Only a few animals feed directly on the coral. Many more either graze on the film of algae that grows on the coral, eat the plankton that drifts past, or hunt larger marine creatures.

A multicolored world

Many of the reef's inhabitants are vividly colored. In many cases, the bright colors and bold patterns indicate that the animal is unpleasant to eat or is actually poisonous. Lionfish, for example, carry venomous spines. In some cases, bold patterns enable members of the same species to recognize each other on the crowded reef. In other instances, the stripes and patterns serve to break up the body outline and thus provide camouflage.

Moorish idol

Sponges, jellyfish, and relatives

Adult sponges have simple bodies and remain in one place, such as on a rock. Sea anemones belong to a group of creatures called cnidarians, as do corals and jellyfish. Most have tentacles with stinging cells. Comb jellies are a separate group. They are small, translucent, and they float in surface waters. Lampshells anchor themselves to rocks or the seafloor by a fleshy stalk.

Lampshell

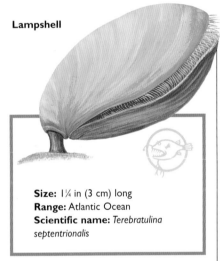

Size: 1¼ in (3 cm) long
Range: Atlantic Ocean
Scientific name: *Terebratulina septentrionalis*

Lampshell

The lampshell belongs to a group of animals called brachiopods. Brachiopods have lived on Earth for more than 550 million years. The lampshell has two shells and a short stalk on which it can move around. When the shells open, they expose folded tentacles lined with tiny hairs. These hairs drive water over the tentacles, which trap tiny particles of food.

Sea anemone

The sea anemone may look like a flower, but it is actually an animal that catches other creatures to eat. At the base of its body is a sucking disk that keeps the anemone attached to a rock. At the top is its mouth, which is surrounded by stinging tentacles.

Size: up to 9¾ in (25 cm) tall
Range: Atlantic and Pacific oceans
Scientific name: *Tealia* spp.

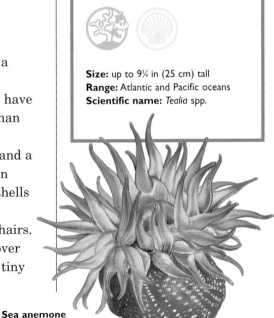

Sea anemone

Common comb jelly

The comb jelly moves with the help of tiny hairs arranged in lines down its baglike body. These hairs are called comb plates, and they beat together to push the comb jelly through the water. It eats shrimp and other small creatures.

Common comb jelly

Size: 6 in (15 cm) long
Range: Arctic and Atlantic oceans
Scientific name: *Bolinopsis infundibulum*

Purple jellyfish

Purple jellyfish

Although known as the purple jellyfish, it may be yellow, red, or even brown. Its stinging cells protect it from enemies and help it to catch food.

Size: bell: 1¼ in (3 cm) wide; tentacles: 35½ in (90 cm) long
Range: Atlantic, Indian, and Pacific oceans
Scientific name: *Pelagia noctiluca*

54

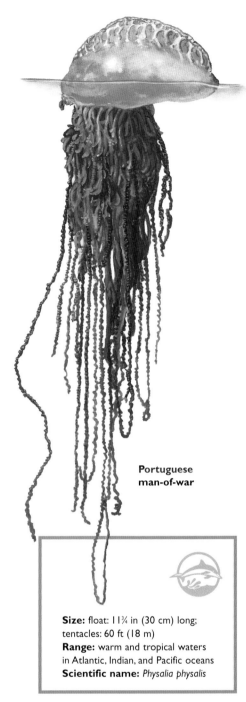

Portuguese man-of-war

Size: 6 in (15 cm) long
Range: Arctic and Atlantic oceans
Scientific name: *Bolinopsis infundibulum*

Vase sponge

Vase sponge

Sponges are among the simplest of animals. To feed, they draw water into the chambers of the body, and tiny particles of food are trapped and digested. The water also provides sponges with oxygen and helps to filter out carbon dioxide.

Sea pen

The feather-like sea pen is not one animal but a group of many individuals called polyps. One large stemlike polyp stands in the seabed and supports the whole group. On the side branches there are many small feeding polyps. If touched, the sea pen glows with phosphorescence.

Sea pen

Size: up to 15 in (38 cm) tall
Range: north Atlantic Ocean
Scientific name: *Pennatula phosphorea*

Brain coral

Brain coral is most common in water 20 to 40 feet (6 to 12 m) deep. Colonies of tiny anemone-like creatures called coral polyps create dome-shaped formations that resemble brains. Each of the polyps has a hard skeleton. These form the rocky base of the colony.

Size: colony up to 6½ ft (2 m) wide
Range: Indian and Pacific oceans, Caribbean Sea, and eastern Atlantic Ocean
Scientific name: *Meandrina spp.*

Size: float: 11¾ in (30 cm) long; tentacles: 60 ft (18 m)
Range: warm and tropical waters in Atlantic, Indian, and Pacific oceans
Scientific name: *Physalia physalis*

Portuguese man-of-war

The Portuguese man-of-war is not a true jellyfish: it is a colony of hundreds of animals called polyps. They live together under the sail-like, gas-filled float, and each polyp performs a different task for the colony, such as capturing food or producing eggs.

Brain coral colony

Crustaceans

There are about 31,000 species of crustaceans, including barnacles, lobsters, shrimp, and crabs. Wood lice live on land, and there are some crustaceans in fresh water, but most live in the sea. Crustaceans are invertebrates and typically have a tough outer skeleton that protects the soft body within. Their head is made up of six segments on which there are two pairs of antennae and several sets of mouthparts. The rest of the body, which may be divided into a thorax and an abdomen, carries the walking legs.

Goose barnacles

Goose barnacles live fixed by their stalks to any object floating in the open sea, such as logs, buoys, and boats. Their body is enclosed by a shell made of five plates, which open at the top so that the barnacle can extend its feathery legs and collect particles of food from the water.

Goose barnacles

Size: 6 in (15 cm) including stalk
Range: Atlantic and Pacific Oceans
Scientific name: *Lepas anatifera*

Size: 11¾ in (30 cm)
Range: north Atlantic coasts
Scientific name: *Homerus americanus*

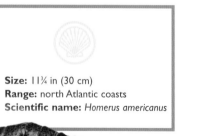

American lobster

American lobster

During the day the lobster hides in rock crevices, but at night it comes out to hunt. In the summer, the female lobster lays thousands of eggs, which it carries in the underside of its tail. These hatch into shrimplike larvae that float on the surface for a few weeks and then settle on the seafloor and develop into adults.

Deep-sea shrimp

The deep-sea shrimp's antennae are longer than its body. It spreads its antennae out in the water to help it find food in the darkness of the deep sea. It eats any dead and decaying matter that it comes across.

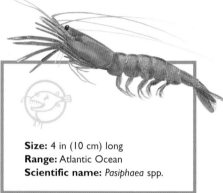

Deep-sea shrimp

Size: 4 in (10 cm) long
Range: Atlantic Ocean
Scientific name: *Pasiphaea* spp.

Giant isopod

A sea-living relative of the wood louse, the giant isopod lives in Antarctic waters, where it catches any food it can find. It also scavenges on the seafloor for dead and dying creatures. Antarctic isopods are among the largest isopods in the world.

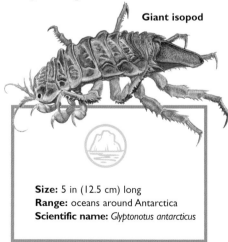

Giant isopod

Size: 5 in (12.5 cm) long
Range: oceans around Antarctica
Scientific name: *Glyptonotus antarcticus*

Hermit crab

Unlike other crabs, the hermit crab has no hard shell of its own. It protects its soft body by living in the discarded shell of another creature, such as a sea snail. The crab has large pincers on its first pair of legs that it uses to grab prey.

Hermit crab

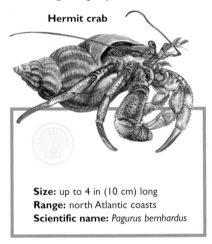

Size: up to 4 in (10 cm) long
Range: north Atlantic coasts
Scientific name: *Pagurus bernhardus*

Montague's shrimp

Shrimp have much thinner shells than crabs or lobsters. The limbs on the abdomen are used for swimming. Some on the thorax are for walking, and others are used as mouthparts.

Montague's shrimp

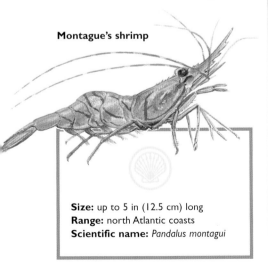

Size: up to 5 in (12.5 cm) long
Range: north Atlantic coasts
Scientific name: *Pandalus montagui*

Antarctic krill

Antarctic krill

Shrimplike krill feed on plant and animal plankton that they sieve from the water. They are the main food of many fish, penguins, and whales. A blue whale can eat up to four million krill in a day. Krill are very common and can occur in such large numbers that the sea looks red.

Size: up to 2 in (5 cm) long
Range: oceans around Antarctica
Scientific name: *Euphausia superba*

Amphipod

This small crustacean lives on the lower shore under rocks or among seaweed and feeds on tiny pieces of plant and animal matter. On its abdomen are three pairs of jumping legs. The female amphipod holds her developing young in a pouch on the underside of her body.

Amphipod

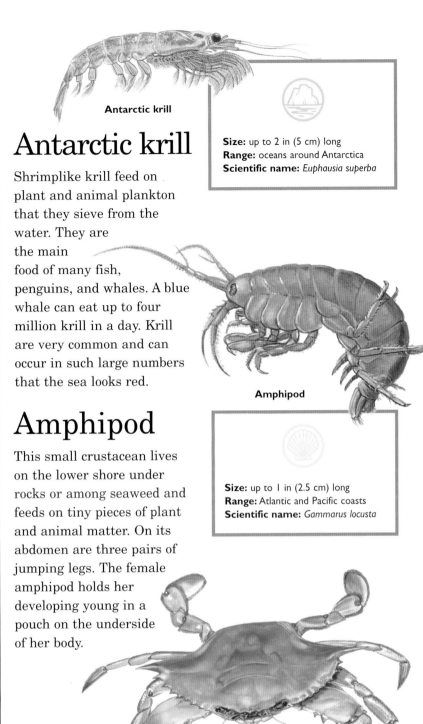

Size: up to 1 in (2.5 cm) long
Range: Atlantic and Pacific coasts
Scientific name: *Gammarus locusta*

Blue crab

Size: 9¼ in (23 cm) wide
Range: Atlantic and Gulf coasts of North America; South America to Uruguay; West Indies
Scientific name: *Callinectes sapidus*

Blue crab

Most crabs have a strong shell that protects the body and five pairs of legs. The first pair has powerful pincers that are used to break open the shells of prey. The blue crab is an extremely popular edible crab.

Mollusks

There are at least 100,000 species of mollusks, many of which are found in the sea. They are divided into three main groups—gastropods, such as limpets and snails; bivalves, such as clams and scallops; and cephalopods, such as squid and octopuses. In most mollusks, the body is divided into the head, which contains the mouth and sense organs; the body; and the foot, a fleshy part on which the animal moves along. Most also have a shell that protects the soft body.

Iceland scallop

Eye

Size: 4 in (10 cm) long
Range: Arctic and North Atlantic oceans
Scientific name: *Chlamys islandicus*

Atlantic deer cowrie

The cowrie is a type of sea snail with a beautiful, shiny shell. Unlike most snails, the cowrie's mantle can be extended to cover the outside of the shell and camouflage the animal. (The mantle is a thin fold of tissue, part of which makes the shell.) The opening of the cowrie's shell is edged with 35 teeth.

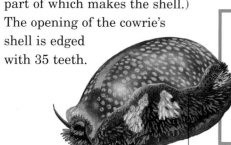

Atlantic deer cowrie   **Mantle**

Iceland scallop

The scallop is a member of the bivalve group of mollusks, and it has a soft body protected by two shells. A row of well-developed eyes can be seen on each shell when the shells are slightly parted. The scallop moves by pulling its shells together, forcing out jets of water to push itself along.

Size: up to 5 in (12.5 cm) long
Range: western Atlantic Ocean and Caribbean Sea
Scientific name: *Cypraea cervus*

Butternut clam

The clam lives in a burrow deep in a sandy or muddy seabed, which it digs with its foot. Two long tubes can be extended from inside the shell. Water and food go in through one tube and then the filtered water goes out of the other tube.

Butternut clam

Size: 6 in (15 cm) long
Range: north Pacific Ocean
Scientific name: *Saxidomus nuttalli*

Eastern oyster

The oyster is a type of bivalve. It has a soft body protected by two hard shells, which are held together by strong muscles. It eats tiny pieces of plant and animal food that it filters from the water. The water is drawn into the partly opened shell, and any food is caught on tiny sticky hairs on the oyster's gills.

Size: up to 4 in (10 cm) long
Range: Atlantic and Gulf coasts of North America
Scientific name: *Crassotrea virginica*

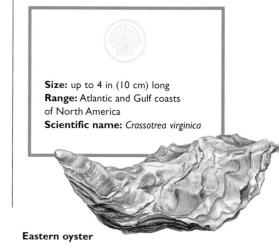

Eastern oyster

Size: up to 40 in (100 cm) long
Range: Atlantic coasts
Scientific name: *Octopus vulgaris*

Common octopus

Common octopus

The octopus has eight long arms, or tentacles, lined with two rows of suckers. It pulls itself along with its strong arms and can also swim quickly by shooting jets of water out of its body. It spends much of its time hiding in crevices or under rocks, watching out for prey, such as crabs, clams, and shrimp. The octopus holds its prey in its tentacles and then may kill or paralyze it with a poisonous bite.

Purple sea snail

This little snail cannot swim, but it drifts in the surface waters of the sea, clinging to a raft of bubbles made from mucus it has secreted. The mucus hardens when it enters the sea.

Lightning whelk

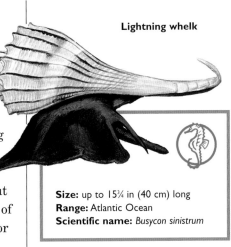

Size: up to 15¾ in (40 cm) long
Range: Atlantic Ocean
Scientific name: *Busycon sinistrum*

Lightning whelk

This large whelk has a very beautiful spiral shell with brown markings. It lives on sandy or muddy seabeds in shallow water and feeds mostly on clams and other mollusks, which it digs out of the seafloor.

Purple sea snail

Size: 1 in (2.5 cm) in diameter
Range: Atlantic, Indian, and Pacific oceans
Scientific name: *Janthina janthina*

Chromodoris nudibranch

Size: 6 in (15 cm) long
Range: Pacific coasts
Scientific name: *Chromodoris elisabethina*

Chromodoris nudibranch

Nudibranchs, or sea slugs, are a group of snails that have no shells. They are often brightly colored. This species has a pair of hornlike projections and a clump of feathery gills on its back. Sponges are its main food.

Longfin inshore squid

The squid has four pairs of arms, one pair of tentacles, and a torpedo-shaped body. Suckers on the arms and tentacles help the squid grasp its prey. The squid moves by shooting water out of its body, which forces it backward through the water.

Size: up to 30 in (76 cm) long, including tentacles
Range: Atlantic Ocean and Mediterranean Sea
Scientific name: *Loligo pealii*

Longfin inshore squid

Worms and echinoderms

There are about 11,500 species of segmented, or annelid, worms. Some live on land or in fresh water, but most live in the sea. All echinoderms live in the sea. There are four main groups: brittle stars, sea stars, sea cucumbers, and sea urchins. Many have a body that is divided into five parts. Most move around using tiny stilts called tube feet, each tipped with a sucking disk.

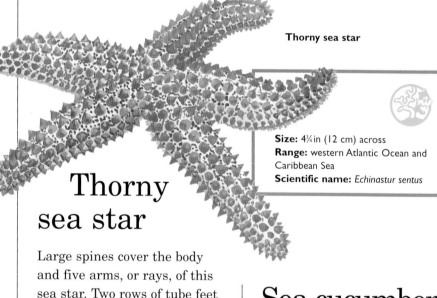

Thorny sea star

Size: 4¾ in (12 cm) across
Range: western Atlantic Ocean and Caribbean Sea
Scientific name: *Echinastur sentus*

Thorny sea star

Large spines cover the body and five arms, or rays, of this sea star. Two rows of tube feet extend down the underside of each arm, which provide suction to help the sea star move and search for food. Some sea stars are strong enough to pull open mussels or scallops.

Sea cucumber

The sea cucumber is related to starfish, but it has a long, simple body. The anus is at one end and the mouth at the other surrounded by food-gathering tentacles. Rows of tiny tube feet run the length of the body.

Size: up to 9¾ in (25 cm) long
Range: north Atlantic Ocean
Scientific name: *Holothuria forskali*

Sea cucumber

Sea mouse

Despite its plump shape, the sea mouse is actually a kind of worm. Its upper side is covered with lots of grayish-brown bristles that give it a furry look and inspire its common name. The sea mouse spends much of its life under mud or sand in shallow water.

Sea mouse

Size: 7 in (18 cm) long
Range: Atlantic and Mediterranean coasts
Scientific name: *Aphrodita aculeata*

Common sand dollar

The sand dollar, a kind of sea urchin, has a shell covered with short bristles. It uses tube feet on the flat underside of its body to gather food as it moves through the sand.

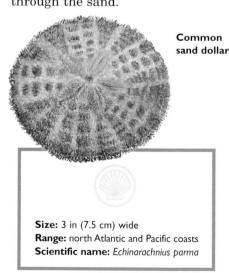

Common sand dollar

Size: 3 in (7.5 cm) wide
Range: north Atlantic and Pacific coasts
Scientific name: *Echinarachnius parma*

Feather-duster worm

This worm's body is usually hidden in a tube attached to a reef or the seabed. The tube is made of fine sand stuck together with a gluey substance made in the worm's body. The worm catches food with its crown of feathery gills.

Tube ——

Feather-duster worm

Size: 5 in (12.5 cm) long
Range: Atlantic Ocean and Caribbean Sea
Scientific name: *Sabellastarte magnifica*

Paddle worm

Size: 17¾ in (45 cm) long
Range: Atlantic and Pacific coasts
Scientific name: *Phyllodoce* spp.

Paddle worm

This worm lives under rocks among seaweed, both on the shore and in deeper water. It has four pairs of tentacles on its head and lots of tiny leaflike paddles down each side of its long body. It feeds mainly on other worms.

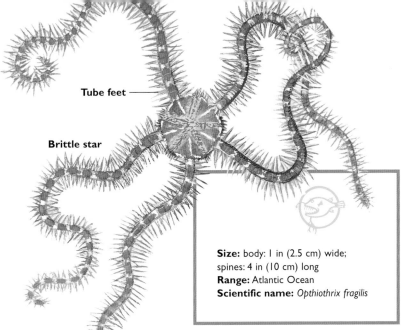

Tube feet ——

Brittle star

Long-spined urchin

Sharp spines protect this sea urchin's body from enemies. The urchin's mouth is on the underside of its body, and it has five teeth in a circle for chewing food. By day it hides on the reef, but at night it comes out to feed on algae.

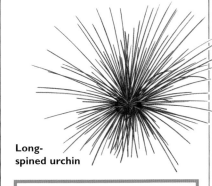

Long-spined urchin

Size: body: 4 in (10 cm) wide; spines: 4–15¾ in (10–40 cm) long
Range: tropical parts of Atlantic Ocean and Caribbean Sea
Scientific name: *Diadema antillarum*

Size: body: 1 in (2.5 cm) wide; spines: 4 in (10 cm) long
Range: Atlantic Ocean
Scientific name: *Opthiothrix fragilis*

Brittle star

The brittle star gets its name because its arms are easily broken off, although they do grow back again. The animal uses its tube feet to catch small crustaceans and other creatures. Its mouth is on the underside of the central disk.

Sea lily

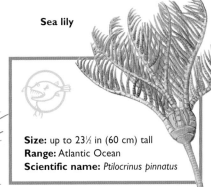

Size: up to 23½ in (60 cm) tall
Range: Atlantic Ocean
Scientific name: *Ptilocrinus pinnatus*

Sea lily

The sea lily lives attached to the seabed by a stalk. Its arms are lined with sucker-like tube feet. To feed, it spreads its arms and traps tiny particles. The food is then passed down grooves lined with hairs to the mouth, at the center of the body.

Whales

Whales are the largest sea mammals. There are two kinds of whales—toothed and baleen. Baleen whales have bristly plates in their mouths instead of teeth. When they feed, they take gulps of water. Baleen plates act as filters, so the water drains out, but the fish and plankton, including krill, stay in the whale's mouth. Toothed whales can locate other sea creatures by echolocation. They send out high-pitched clicking sounds and detect the echoes as they bounce back from objects.

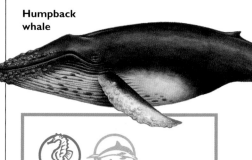

Size: 26–33 ft (8–10 m)
Range: temperate and polar areas of all oceans
Scientific name: *Balaenoptera acutorostrata*

Minke whale

This baleen whale is a pint-size relative of the humpback and blue whales. Like them, the minke has distinctive grooves along its throat. In polar regions, the minke feeds mainly on krill, but in warmer waters, it also eats fish and squid.

Blue whale

Blue whale

The world's largest mammal, the blue whale can weigh up to 215 tons. This giant baleen whale feeds on huge quantities of tiny creatures called krill, consuming 4 to 8 tons each day in the summer. The blue whale is in danger of extinction, and only a few thousand are left in the world's oceans.

Size: 82–105 ft (25–32 m)
Range: all oceans
Scientific name: *Balaenoptera musculus*

Gray whale

This whale stirs up the seabed with its snout and uses its baleen to filter out tiny creatures to eat. It makes a round trip of 12,430 miles (20,000 km) between its summer feeding waters off Alaska and the warmer, shallower waters off the coast of Mexico, where it breeds during winter.

Humpback whale

The humpback whale is famous for the amazingly complex songs it sings to keep in touch with other humpbacks and to attract mates. This baleen whale often sings for hours on end, pausing only to breathe. These songs can be heard great distances away under water.

Humpback whale

Size: 48–62 ft (15–19 m)
Range: all oceans
Scientific name: *Megaptera novaeangliae*

Size: 40–50 ft (12.2–15.3 m)
Range: northeastern and northwestern Pacific Ocean
Scientific name: *Eschrichtius robustus*

Gray whale

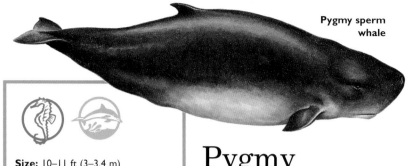
Pygmy sperm
whale

Sperm whale

This toothed whale's huge head is filled with a waxy substance called spermaceti which is thought to help it alter its buoyancy (ability to float). This enables it to reach depths of more than 3,000 feet (1,000 m) in search of squid to eat.

Size: 10–11 ft (3–3.4 m)
Range: all oceans
Scientific name: *Kogia breviceps*

Sperm whale

Size: 36–66 ft (11–20 m)
Range: all oceans
Scientific name: *Physeter catodon*

Sei whale

The sei whale is streamlined and flat-headed. It can achieve speeds of 26 mph (50 km/h). It eats almost any kind of plankton, as well as fish and squid, usually feeding near the surface. Family groups of 5 or 6 whales are common. Pair bonds are strong and may last for years. A sei whale calf is fed by its mother for 6 months after birth.

Size: 49–65½ ft (15–20 m)
Range: all oceans
Scientific name:
Balaenoptera borealis

Pygmy sperm whale

Its underslung lower jaw gives the pygmy sperm whale an almost shark-like appearance, despite its blunt, square head. Its head accounts for only about 15 percent of its total length. There are 12 or more pairs of teeth in its lower jaw. Short, broad flippers are located far forward, near the head. The body tapers behind the small dorsal fin. Pygmy sperm whales are thought to be shy, slow-moving animals. They feed on squid, fish, and crabs in both deep and shallow water.

Bowhead whale

The bowhead has a massive head and a body that tapers sharply toward the tail. Its jaws are strongly curved to accommodate the 15-foot-long (4.5 m) baleen plates—the longest found on any of the filter-feeding whales. Bowheads feed on the smallest planktonic crustaceans, which they capture on the fine fringes of their baleen.

Size: 49–65 ft (15–20 m)
Range: Arctic Ocean
Scientific name: *Balaena mysticetus*

Bowhead whale

Sei whale

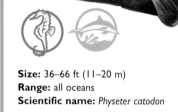

Narwhal

Size: 13–20 ft (4–6 m)
Range: Arctic Ocean
Scientific name: *Monodon monoceros*

White whale

White whale

White whales, also known as belugas, often live together in small groups called pods. They communicate with a variety of sounds, such as whistles, clicks, clangs, twitters, and moos. Polar bears prey on belugas, which get trapped by the Arctic ice. In the winter, big herds of belugas migrate south.

Size: 13–20 ft (4–6 m)
Range: Arctic Ocean and subarctic waters
Scientific name: *Delphinapterus leucas*

Narwhal

The narwhal is related to the white whale. It has only two teeth. In males, one of the teeth grows into a spiral tusk up to 9 feet (3 m) long, which sticks through its top lip. The tusk is probably used to impress females and fight rivals during the breeding season. Females sometimes have short tusks.

Goose-beaked whale

Northern bottlenose whale

Size: 21–23 ft (6.4–7 m)
Range: all oceans, temperate and tropical waters
Scientific name: *Ziphius cavirostris*

Northern bottlenose whale

Sturdy and round-bodied, the northern bottlenose has a prominent, bulbous forehead. Males are generally larger than females. Squid and some fish, such as herring and sometimes sea stars, make up this whale's main diet. A member of a deep-diving family, the bottlenose is believed to dive to greater

Size: 24–33 ft (7.3–10 m)
Range: Arctic and north Atlantic oceans
Scientific name: *Hyperoodon ampullatus*

depths than any other whale. It also remains under water longer than any other whale. Populations have been reduced by commercial whaling.

Goose-beaked whale

This is one of 18 toothed whale species with a distinct beak. It has a tapering, scarred body marked by oval patches where parasitic lampreys have fed on it. It dives for up to 30 minutes to feed on squid and deep-water fish.

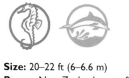

Sowerby's beaked whale

There are 12 closely related species of beaked whale in the genus Mesoplodon. Most species tend to live in deep water, so they are rarely seen, and their habits are little-known. All have fairly rounded bodies with small flippers in relation to their body size. Males are larger than females. Sowerby's beaked whale was the first beaked whale to be officially recognized, in 1804. The male has a pointed tooth at each side of the lower jaw. Females either have smaller teeth in this position or no visible teeth at all. Squid and small fish are this whale's main food.

Shepherd's beaked whale

Shepherd's beaked whale was not discovered until 1933, and very few individuals have ever been sighted. Until recently, the species was believed to occur only around New Zealand, but in the 1970s, specimens were found off Argentina and Chile.

Shepherd's beaked whale

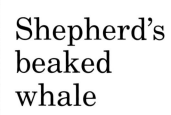

Size: 20–22 ft (6–6.6 m)
Range: New Zealand seas; off coasts of Argentina and Chile
Scientific name: *Tasmacetus shepherdi*

Shepherd's beaked whale has a unique tooth pattern—a pair of large teeth at the tip of its lower jaw, with 12 or more pairs behind them, and about 10 pairs in the upper jaw.

Baird's beaked whale

Baird's is the largest of the beaked whales. This whale's lower jaw has a pair of large teeth sticking out at the tip. The lower jaw extends beyond the upper jaw. Females are larger than males and lighter in color, but they have smaller teeth. Adult males are usually marked with scars, probably caused by battles with other males. Baird's whales are deep divers and feed on squid, fish, octopus, lobster, crabs, and other invertebrates.

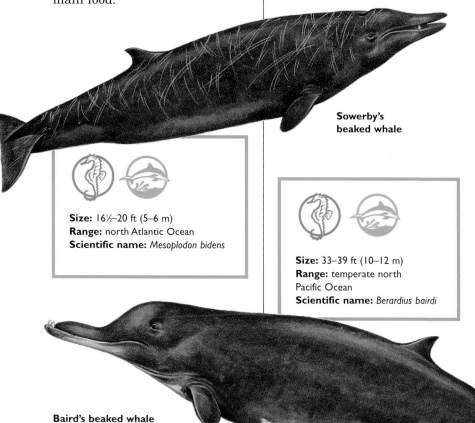

Sowerby's beaked whale

Size: 16½–20 ft (5–6 m)
Range: north Atlantic Ocean
Scientific name: *Mesoplodon bidens*

Size: 33–39 ft (10–12 m)
Range: temperate north Pacific Ocean
Scientific name: *Berardius bairdi*

Baird's beaked whale

65

Endangered species

What happens to the oceans affects our weather and climate, the food we eat, and the air we breathe. Plants in the ocean produce about half of the world's oxygen, while fish are a vital food source. However, human activities are threatening the world's oceans, and thousands of marine animals are at risk of extinction.

Drift net

Purse seiner

Fish in gill net

Trawling
Modern trawlers are able to haul in enormous amounts of fish. Drift nets can be left unattended for long periods of time to trap fish before a trawler returns to collect the catch. With purse seiner nets, a shoal of fish is surrounded by a net which is closed and then pulled on board where the catch is sorted.

Cannery Row, Monterey Bay
In the 1930s, thirty businesses processed fish here. In the 1950s, many closed down when the California sardine stocks collapsed.

Overfishing

For hundreds of years, fishermen have been overfishing, thus depleting one fish population after another. This means that too many fish are removed from the water, so they cannot replace their numbers quickly enough and the numbers of fish decline. The Food and Agriculture Organization of the United Nations (FAO) estimates that 13 of the world's major fish populations are being overfished.

Inuit whalers butcher a bowhead whale. Some traditional communities are allowed to kill a few whales each year.

Overhunting

By the early 1900s, whaling had made some whale species nearly extinct, so European and North American sailors traveled to the Antarctic Ocean to hunt the whales there. Slow-moving humpback whales were hunted first, then the largest whales—blue and fin. When these populations were exhausted, smaller whales—sei and minke—were hunted. In 1986, when many whale populations were dangerously low, a worldwide ban on whaling was introduced. Despite international objections, Norway and Japan still catch several hundred whales a year. However, several whale populations are gradually recovering.

A selection of endangered or extinct sea creatures	
Endangered species	**Cause**
Salmon and sturgeon	Salmon and sturgeon are very tasty fish, so they have a high value. They migrate between river and sea, and are endangered by dam-building, overfishing, and pollution.
Seahorse	Thirty-one species of seahorse are endangered because of collecting. Their dried bodies are sold as souvenirs or ground up for use in traditional medicines.
Steller's sea cow	After being discovered in the Bering Sea in 1741, this sea mammal was hunted to extinction within 30 years. Its flesh was said to be "as good as the best cuts of beef." The sea cow was related to dugongs and manatees.
Northern right whale	After being hunted for 800 years before being protected in 1935, the population has failed to recover. Only 300 to 400 survive. These slow-moving coastal whales are endangered by inbreeding, collisions with ships, and getting tangled in fishing nets.
Vaquita	This very small porpoise is found only at the northern end of the Gulf of California. Probably fewer than 500 remain. Pollution, entanglement in nets, and illegal hunting threaten their survival.
West Indian manatee	The West Indian manatee, a species of sea cow, has been reduced to a population of less than 2,000. Individuals are threatened by coastal pollution, and more than a hundred die each year in collisions with speedboats.

Seahorse

Vaquita

Sturgeon

Salmon

West Indian manatee

Northern right whale

Extinction

In the sea, as well as on land, animals and plants are dying out at an increasing rate because of human interference. Humans pollute the sea, alter or destroy marine habitats, and hunt sea creatures to the edge of extinction. The loss of large animals gains more attention, but many small creatures are probably becoming extinct before scientists have even had time to study them.

This painting shows Steller's sea cows. This species was hunted to extinction within 30 years of its discovery by European sailors.

The future

There is some good news for endangered species. Scientific organizations such as the Intergovernmental Panel on Climate Change (IPCC) are bringing air pollution and global warming to the attention of governments. There are now more than 1,300 protected marine areas. Since 1994 the use of the oceans is governed by an international Law of the Sea treaty.

Dolphins and porpoises

Like whales, dolphins and porpoises are cetaceans. Cetaceans are aquatic mammals with a nearly hairless body and paddle-shaped front limbs. Typically, dolphins have bulging foreheads containing the melon—a pad of fat thought to help focus their sonar beams. Porpoises are small, beakless whales. They are usually shorter than 7 feet (2 m) in length, and they generally have prominent dorsal fins.

Killer whale

Although it is called a "whale," the killer whale is actually the largest of the dolphin family. Also known as an orca, it is a fierce hunter that feeds on fish, squid, sea lions, seabirds, and even other whales. It sometimes snatches seals from the shore or knocks them off floating ice and into its mouth.

Size: 23–32 ft (7–9.7 m)
Range: worldwide, especially cooler seas
Scientific name: *Orcinus orca*

Common dolphin

This beautifully marked dolphin has pointed flippers, a curved fin, and a long beak. It lives in groups of between 20 and 100 dolphins. Several dolphins may join together to help injured or sick companions. These curious, playful sea mammals are often seen swimming alongside ships, leaping and rolling in the waves. They feed on fish and squid.

Size: 7–8½ ft (2.1–2.6 m)
Range: warm and tropical oceans worldwide
Scientific name: *Delphinus delphis*

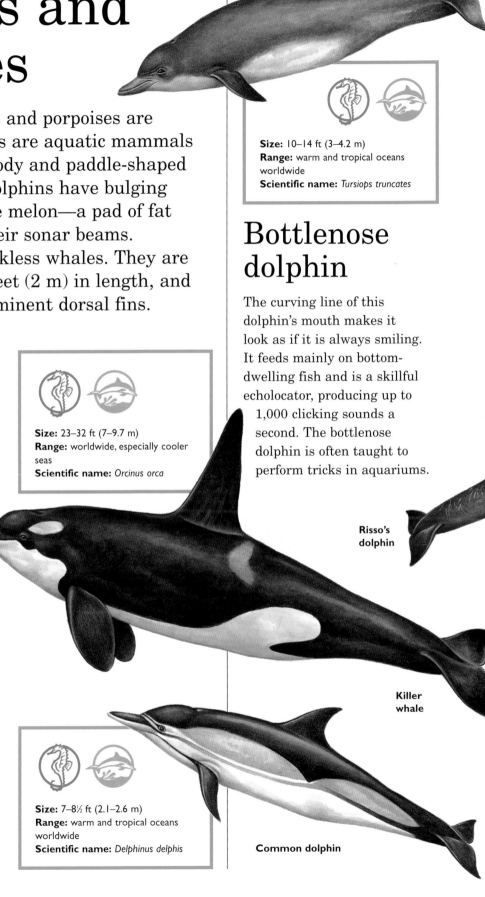

Bottlenose dolphin

Size: 10–14 ft (3–4.2 m)
Range: warm and tropical oceans worldwide
Scientific name: *Tursiops truncates*

Bottlenose dolphin

The curving line of this dolphin's mouth makes it look as if it is always smiling. It feeds mainly on bottom-dwelling fish and is a skillful echolocator, producing up to 1,000 clicking sounds a second. The bottlenose dolphin is often taught to perform tricks in aquariums.

Risso's dolphin

Killer whale

Common dolphin

Long-finned pilot whale

Size: 16–28 ft (5–8.5 m)
Range: north Atlantic Ocean; temperate southern oceans
Scientific name: *Globicephala melaena*

Long-finned pilot whale

The long-finned pilot whale is a member of the dolphin family. It has an unusual square-shaped head and long, narrow flippers. Squid is this whale's main food, but it also feeds on fish. The range of this species is unusual in that it occurs in two widely separated areas.

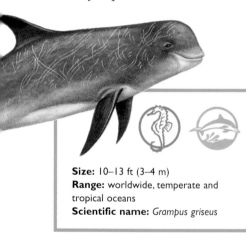

Size: 10–13 ft (3–4 m)
Range: worldwide, temperate and tropical oceans
Scientific name: *Grampus griseus*

Risso's dolphin

This dolphin's body is broad in front of the fin and tapers off behind it. Adults often have scars caused by fighting. The Risso's dolphin has a crease down the center of its forehead to the lip. Its upper jaw is toothless, but there are up to eight teeth in the lower jaw.

Indo-pacific humpbacked dolphin

Size: 6½–10 ft (2–3 m)
Range: Indian Ocean, southwest Pacific Ocean, Yangtze River
Scientific name: *Sousa chinensis*

Striped dolphin

The coloration of this species varies, but there is always a dark stripe running along the side and usually a dark band curving from the dorsal fin toward the eye. Striped dolphins have between 90 and 100 teeth and feed on small fish, squid, and shrimp. They move in large schools of several hundred, even several thousand. Females breed about every three years and the gestation period is one year. Calves are nursed by their mothers for 9 to 18 months.

Indo-Pacific humpbacked dolphin

The young of this species all have a streamlined body shape, but adults have humps of fatty tissue on their back. This dolphin's beak is long, and there are a total of at least 120 teeth. These dolphins feed in shallow water on fish, mollusks, and crustaceans and use echolocation when searching for prey. They are sociable creatures, living in groups of up to 20.

Size: 8–10 ft (2.4–3 m)
Range: Atlantic and Pacific oceans, temperate and tropical areas
Scientific name: *Stenella coeruleoalba*

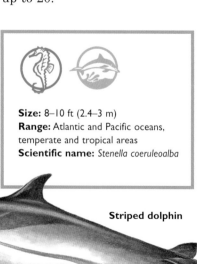
Striped dolphin

Finless porpoise

Harbor porpoise

These porpoises feed on fish such as herring and mackerel. They dive for up to six minutes when hunting prey, which they pinpoint using echolocation clicks. Before breeding, they perform long courtship rituals, caressing each other as they swim side by side. Calves are born 10 to 11 months after mating. While a mother suckles her calf, she lies on her side on the water surface, so the calf can breathe easily.

Harbor porpoise

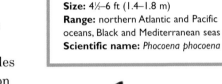

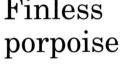

Size: 4½–6 ft (1.4–1.8 m)
Range: east and southeast Asia: Pakistan to Borneo and Korea; Yangtze River, east China Sea
Scientific name: *Neophocaena phocaenoides*

Size: 4½–6 ft (1.4–1.8 m)
Range: northern Atlantic and Pacific oceans, Black and Mediterranean seas
Scientific name: *Phocoena phocoena*

Finless porpoise

The finless porpoise looks different from other porpoises. Its forehead sticks out and is quite round, which gives the appearance of a slight beak. It has a ridge of small, rounded projections just behind where the dorsal fin should be. Finless porpoises dive for less than a minute in search of prey and are quick and agile in the water. They feed largely on crustaceans, squid, and fish, and are skilful echolocators. Finless porpoises usually move in pairs, although groups of up to ten are sometimes seen. Little is known of their breeding behavior, but young calves travel clinging to the projections on their mothers' backs.

Dall's porpoise

Size: 6–7½ ft (1.8–2.3 m)
Range: warm northern Pacific waters
Scientific name: *Phocoenides dalli*

Dall's porpoise

These porpoises are larger and heavier than most porpoises and inhabit deeper waters. They live in groups of up to 15. Schools of 100 or more porpoises may gather to migrate north in summer and south in winter. Mothers suckle their calves for as long as two years.

Size: 7½–8 ft (2.3–2.5m)
Range: north Pacific Ocean
Scientific name: *Lagenorynchus obliquidens*

Pacific white-sided dolphin

The chin, throat, and belly of the Pacific white-sided dolphin are creamy-white, while the beak, flippers, back, and dorsal fin are dark gray. It has light gray patches on the sides and a light gray stripe from above the eye to below the dorsal fin. It is active and friendly—it often approaches boats. It lives in groups of about 90 individuals, but supergroups of more than 3,000 have been known.

Pacific white-sided dolphin

70

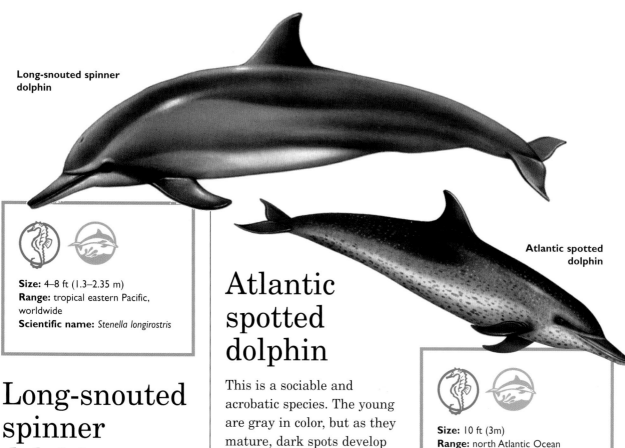

Long-snouted spinner dolphin

Atlantic spotted dolphin

Size: 4–8 ft (1.3–2.35 m)
Range: tropical eastern Pacific, worldwide
Scientific name: *Stenella longirostris*

Long-snouted spinner dolphin

The spinner is a small, dark gray dolphin with darker patches on the tail, back, and throat. Most also have creamy-white patches on the belly. Spinners live in groups ranging from just a few to schools of thousands. They are famous for leaping through the air and spinning. It is thought that this is either to attract other individuals in the school or simply for fun.

Atlantic spotted dolphin

This is a sociable and acrobatic species. The young are gray in color, but as they mature, dark spots develop on their bellies and white spots appear on their flanks. As they grow, more spots appear, so that adults are black with white spots.

Size: 7–8 ft (2.2–2.5 m)
Range: temperate and tropical areas of the Atlantic Ocean
Scientific name: *Stenella frontalis*

Size: 10 ft (3m)
Range: north Atlantic Ocean
Scientific name: *Lagenorhynchus albirostris*

White-beaked dolphin

This dolphin has a short, thick, creamy-white beak and a curved dorsal fin. It is often confused with the white-sided dolphin, but the white-beaked is larger and does not have yellow streaks on its side. White-beaked dolphins are friendly and acrobatic animals. They can be found riding on the waves caused by speed boats, and like to feed with other species, such as orca and humpback whales, as well as other dolphins.

White-beaked dolphin

The Seashore

Land and ocean meet at the seashore, where waves crash over rocks or creep up on sandy beaches. A huge range of fish, mammals, reptiles, and invertebrates live in the waters bordering the shore, while others are adapted to live on the shore itself. Coastal birds, such as gulls, gannets, and cormorants, do not spend much time in the water, but they still depend on the sea for food.

Because the tides come in and out twice a day, creatures that live on the seashore have difficult lives—some of the day they are plunged under water, while at other times, they are exposed to the sun and wind. Many shore-dwellers shelter in burrows or under rocks, finding a variety of ways to hold on when waves break over them.

Like most penguins, these king penguins live around the Antarctic. They have to survive freezing conditions and have a dense covering of glossy, waterproof feathers, which keeps them both warm and dry.

Weddell seal

73

Life at the sea's edge

The shore—where land and sea meet—is a difficult environment for animals and plants to live in. Water levels rise and fall with the tides, so shore dwellers find themselves alternately covered in seawater and exposed to the air. They must cope with being baked by the sun and then, a few hours later, being battered by the waves.

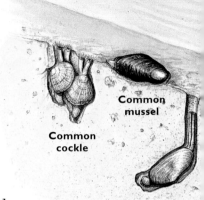

Common cockle

Common mussel

Sand gaper

A rocky existence

The animals and plants that live on rocky shores must withstand or avoid the battering from waves and strong currents. Mussels, limpets, barnacles, and seaweed attach themselves to rocks using strong holdfasts. Crabs and small snails, along with other marine creatures, escape to the shelter of cracks, crevices, and rockpools. The shore also provides a rich feeding ground for its inhabitants. Mussels and barnacles filter the seawater to extract a plankton feast. Limpets and snails graze the algae that grow on rocks. Larger snails, known as dogwhelks, drill holes in barnacle shells and digest the contents.

Various communities of animals and plants live at different levels on the shore. Depending on their position, they adapt to survive under particular conditions—for example, longer exposure to the air if they are higher up the shoreline. Shallow waters close to the shore are filled with fish and invertebrates.

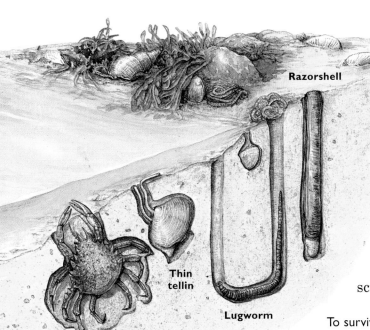

Razorshell

Thin tellin

Lugworm

Spider crab

Beach life

The sandy shore can be a hostile environment for small creatures, which cannot grip the fine particles of sand to stop themselves being washed away. However, there are countless burrowing animals living below the surface. When tidal waters rise and cover the sand, many of the creatures extend their legs or tentacles into the water to feed. They filter the water for plankton or scratch at the sandy surface, seeking food.

To survive on a sandy shore, many animals burrow below the sand.

Forests in the sea

In cool, shallow waters where the sea bottom is rocky, huge seaweed called kelp grow in abundance. Their fronds reach many yards in length and create a dense underwater forest that extends from the seafloor to the surface. Kelp can grow as much as 20 inches (50 cm) in a day. Tiny plants and animals grow on the kelp. Lobsters, sea stars, crabs, worms, and fish hunt, graze, and forage in and around the kelp forest and are in turn the prey of seals and sea

Hatching time

Reptiles that live in the ocean need to come ashore to lay their eggs. Every year turtles swim thousands of miles to find the right beach for their nests. Green turtles will crawl up a beach to a point above the high-tide mark. Here, they dig a small hole in the sand using all four of their flippers. The female then lays the eggs carefully into the nest before covering them with sand and returning to the sea.

After hatching, young turtles have to scurry to the sea. At this time, they are very vulnerable and many are eaten by predators.

Reptiles

Today there are more than 6,500 known species of reptiles. Most reptiles live on land, but there are species in all of the world's oceans, except for the seas around Antarctica. The eggs of reptiles are surrounded by a tough shell, which means they can be laid on land. Many eggs hatch in buried nests where the earth keeps them warm during development.

Size: up to 27 ft (9 m)
Range: southern India, Indonesia, southern Australia
Scientific name: *Crocodylus porosus*

Saltwater crocodile

Saltwater crocodile

This is one of the largest and most dangerous of all crocodiles. It has been known to attack humans. It spends much of its life in the sea, catching fish, but it also preys on land animals such as monkeys, cattle, and buffalo. The female comes to land to lay up to 80 eggs in a mound of plant material.

Leatherback

The world's largest sea turtle, the leatherback, weighs about 800 pounds (360 kg) and feeds mostly on jellyfish. Its shell is made of a thick, leathery material. Leatherbacks travel long distances between their feeding and nesting sites. Most breed every other year and lay up to nine clutches (groups of eggs). Newly hatched young have scales on their shells and skin.

Leatherback

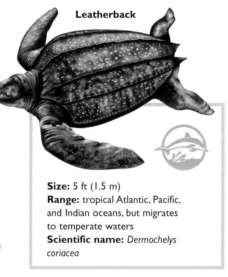

Size: 5 ft (1.5 m)
Range: tropical Atlantic, Pacific, and Indian oceans, but migrates to temperate waters
Scientific name: *Dermochelys coriacea*

Hawksbill

Size: 30–36 in (76–91 cm)
Range: tropical Atlantic, Pacific, and Indian oceans, Caribbean
Scientific name: *Eretmochelys imbricata*

Hawksbill

Hawksbills have long been hunted for their shells, as well as for their eggs. There are now strict controls on hunting, but numbers are still low. This sea turtle has an unusual diet. In addition to eating mollusks and crustaceans, it feeds on sponges. Many of these contain poisons, but the toxins do not affect the turtles.

Size: 30–80 in (76–200 cm)
Range: temperate and tropical areas of Pacific, Indian, and Atlantic oceans, Mediterranean Sea
Scientific name: *Caretta caretta*

Loggerhead

Like most sea turtles, breeding loggerheads return to the same beaches where they hatched. Females dig holes in the sand and lay about 100 eggs. Two months later, hatchlings dig out and run to the water, but many are eaten by birds. Others, attracted by lights on the shore, wander away from the sea and die.

Loggerhead

Atlantic green turtle

This turtle spends most of its life in the sea, feeding on seaweed and sea grasses. A female lays her eggs on the beach where she was born. She digs a pit, lays 100 or more eggs, covers them with sand, and returns to the sea. When the young hatch, they must struggle out of the pit and down to the sea.

Size: 3¼–4 ft (1–1.25 m)
Range: tropical Atlantic, Pacific, and Indian oceans
Scientific name: *Chelonia mydas*

Marine iguana

The marine iguana is the only lizard that spends most of its life in the sea, swimming and diving as it searches for algae, which it scrapes off rocks and eats. When in the water, the iguana uses its powerful tail to push itself along. It has to come to the surface to breathe, but when it dives, its heart rate slows so its body uses less oxygen.

Size: 4–5 ft (1.2–1.5 m)
Range: Galápagos Islands
Scientific name: *Amblyrhynchus cristatus*

Banded sea snake

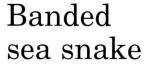

This snake spends all its life in the sea, never going on land. Its body is slightly flattened, and its paddle-shaped tail helps it move through the water. It breathes air but can stay underwater for up to two hours. Like all sea snakes, it eats fish and has a poisonous bite.

Banded sea snake

Size: 6½ ft (2 m)
Range: coastal areas of Indian and Pacific oceans
Scientific name: *Hydrophis cyanocinctus*

Atlantic green turtle

Size: 26 in (66 cm)
Range: tropical Pacific, Indian and south Atlantic oceans
Scientific name: *Lepidochelys olivacea*

Pacific ridley turtle

The Pacific ridley is small and lightly built for a sea turtle. It feeds on small shrimp, jellyfish, crabs, snails, and fish, which it crushes with strong jaws. The Pacific ridley breeds every year and always returns to the same nesting beaches. The female lays about 100 eggs in a pit in the sand and covers them. She then begins a strange movement—rocking from side to side so that each edge of the shell thumps the sand in turn.

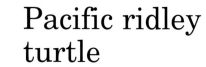

Pacific ridley turtle

Marine iguana

Seals

Seals are carnivorous. Their diet consists mainly of fish, shellfish, squid, and other marine creatures. Seals have a large, sleek body which tapers off into a narrow tail. Instead of arms and legs, seals have flippers. These flippers are ideally suited to swimming but make moving on land a little awkward. Seals also use their flippers to communicate—they "talk" to each other by slapping the water and grunting. The largest seal is the elephant seal, which can weigh up to 2 tons (1.8 tonnes).

Harbor seal

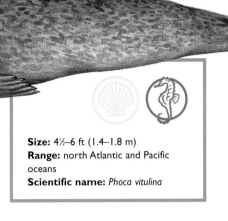

Size: 4½–6 ft (1.4–1.8 m)
Range: north Atlantic and Pacific oceans
Scientific name: *Phoca vitulina*

Harbor seal

Like all seals, the harbor seal spends most of its life in the ocean, coming to land only to mate and give birth. Harbor seal pups are well developed when they are born. They can swim from birth and can dive for up to two minutes when just two or three days old. The harbor seal feeds on fish and squid.

Leopard seal

The leopard seal is the fiercest hunter of all seals, with large tooth-studded jaws for grasping prey and tearing it apart. The leopard seal preys on penguins by catching them underwater just after they dive off the ice. It also hunts smaller seals as well as fish, squid, and shellfish.

Gray seal

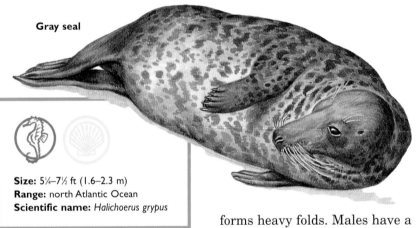

Size: 5¼–7½ ft (1.6–2.3 m)
Range: north Atlantic Ocean
Scientific name: *Halichoerus grypus*

Gray seal

Male gray seals weigh up to 660 pounds (300 kg) and are up to twice as heavy as females. The male's massive shoulders are covered with thick skin that forms heavy folds. Males have a long snout, rounded forehead, and a wide muzzle. The female has a flatter profile and a more slender muzzle. Gray seals stay mostly in coastal waters, feeding on fish and also on some crustaceans, squid, and octopus.

Leopard seal

Size: 10–11½ ft (3–3.5 m)
Range: seas surrounding Antarctica
Scientific name: *Hydrurga leptonyx*

Harp seal

The harp seal feeds on fish and crustaceans. In the breeding season, rival males fight over females, using their teeth and flippers. After mating, the females form groups on the ice to give birth. The pups grow rapidly as they feed on their mother's nourishing fat-rich milk.

Size: 5¼–6¼ ft (1.6–1.9 m)
Range: north Atlantic and Arctic oceans
Scientific name: *Pagophilus groenlandicus*

Mediterranean monk seal

The Mediterranean monk seal is becoming increasingly rare. Its previously remote habitats on islets and cliffs are now more easily reached by humans with their motor boats and scuba diving equipment. The seals often become entangled in fishing nets and can become extremely upset by any disturbance. Mothers and pregnant females, in particular, are nervous of any approach.

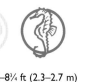

Size: 7½–8¾ ft (2.3–2.7 m)
Range: west Atlantic Ocean: Canary Islands to Mediterranean Sea; Turkish coast of Black Sea
Scientific name: *Monachus monachus*

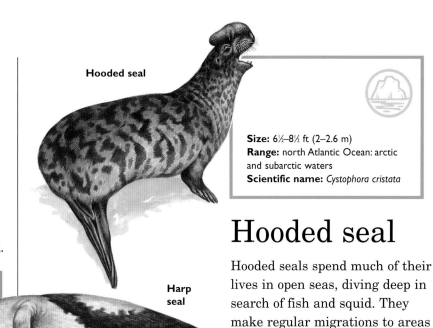

Hooded seal

Harp seal

Size: 6½–8½ ft (2–2.6 m)
Range: north Atlantic Ocean: arctic and subarctic waters
Scientific name: *Cystophora cristata*

Hooded seal

Hooded seals spend much of their lives in open seas, diving deep in search of fish and squid. They make regular migrations to areas of pack ice in the Denmark Strait and east of Greenland. On the pack ice, the adults gather to molt. After molting, the seals part, meeting at breeding grounds in different areas the following spring.

Bearded seal

Long bristles on its snout give the bearded seal its name. It has a heavy build, with females slightly longer than males. Its main foods are bottom-dwelling invertebrates, such as crustaceans, mollusks, and fish. In the breeding season, the males call underwater to attract females.

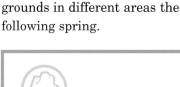

Size: 6¾–7¾ ft (2.1–2.4 m)
Range: Arctic Ocean
Scientific name: *Erignathus barbatus*

Bearded seal

Mediterranean monk seal

Antarctic seals

Antarctica is the world's coldest and most remote continent, and most of it is permanently covered in thick ice. Even the surrounding seas freeze over. With wind speeds sometimes above 200 mph (320 km/h) and temperatures as low as -128°F (-89°C), the Antarctic is so inhospitable that few animals can survive there. However, the seas are rich in food and are able to support a variety of animals, including seals. There are several species of Antarctic seals—the southern elephant, Ross, leopard, crabeater, Weddell, and southern fur seals. For hundreds of years, seals have been killed for their fur and blubber. Some species nearly became extinct but are now recovering. Seals give birth in late winter. By late spring the pups are strong enough to find their own food in the Antarctic waters.

Crabeater seal

Despite their name crabeater seals do not eat crabs. They feed on small, shrimplike creatures called krill, which they filter from the water through their teeth. They detect nearby krill with their long, downward-curving whiskers. Crabeater seals can move as fast as 16 mph (25 km/h) on land. Killer whales often attack these seals.

Elephant seal

The southern elephant seal is the world's largest seal, with males weighing up to 8,800 pounds (4,000 kg). In the breeding season, a male southern elephant seal guards a group of 40 to 50 females, with which he mates. He fights off rival males in fierce battles. A female elephant seal gives birth to a single pup, which she suckles for about a month. During this period the mother does not eat—she lives off the energy stored in her blubber.

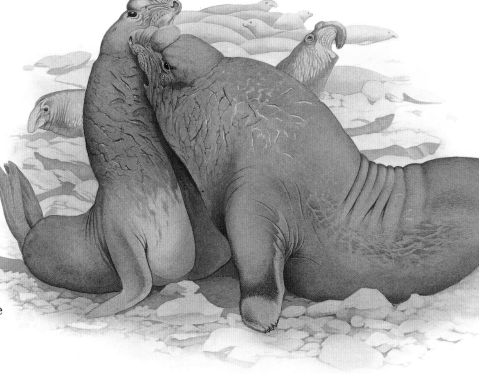

Weddell seal

The Weddell seal makes longer, deeper dives than any other seal, regularly reaching depths of 1,000 to 1,300 feet (300–400 m) in order to feed on Antarctic cod. One Weddell seal was recorded as diving to 2,000 feet (600 m) for 73 minutes. In summer these large, gentle seals spend many hours asleep on the ice. In winter they tend to stay underwater to avoid the harsh conditions, breathing through holes in the ice.

Weddell seal pups are born on the ice during the Antarctic spring. At birth a pup weighs about 55 pounds (25 kg). It grows quickly, nourished by its mother's rich milk, and doubles its weight in about ten days. A pup first enters the water when about six weeks old to start learning to find its own food.

Ross seal

The Ross seal is the smallest—at only 7½ feet (2.3 m)—and rarest Antarctic seal, with a population of perhaps 50,000. This seal is gray along its back and sides and silvery gray to white underneath. It has large eyes, needlelike incisor teeth, and long flippers. It feeds on squid, fish, and krill.

Sea lions, walruses, and sirenians

California sea lion

Size: 5½–7¼ ft (1.7–2.2 m)
Range: Pacific coast from Canada to Mexico
Scientific name: *Zalophus californianus*

Sea lions and fur seals belong to the same family (pinniped) as seals and share similar characteristics. Walruses divide their time between the sea and beaches or ice floes, where they like to gather in large groups. Sirenians, such as manatees and dugongs, live in rivers, estuaries, and coastal seas.

California sea lion

This is the fastest swimmer of all the seals and sea lions, capable of speeds of 25 mph (40 km/h). It can also move fast on land by turning its back flippers forward and lifting its body. In the breeding season, huge colonies gather on the rocky southwestern shores of the United States.

Walrus

Walruses live in the Arctic, where they feed on shellfish. They have sharp tusks, which they use to drag themselves out of the water and also for fighting. Their four flat flippers make them excellent swimmers. On land, walruses move with great difficulty. They spend much of their time sleeping on the ice in large groups.

Walrus

Size: 7¼–11½ ft (2.2–3.5 m)
Range: Arctic, north Atlantic, and north Pacific oceans
Scientific name: *Odobenus rosmarus*

Size: 7¾–9¼ ft (2.4–2.8 m)
Range: north Pacific Ocean
Scientific name: *Eumetopias jubatus*

South American fur seal

South American fur seal

This sea lion eats fish, squid, penguins, and small marine creatures. The female gives birth to a single pup. She stays with it for 12 days and then goes off to sea to feed, returning regularly to suckle her young pup.

Size: 4½–6 ft (1.4–1.8 m)
Range: Pacific and Atlantic coasts of South America
Scientific name: *Arctocephalus australis*

Steller sea lion

Steller sea lion

This largest of the sea lions catches fish, squid, and octopus. A large male may even eat small seals. A sea lion mother goes to sea to find food. When she comes back, she makes a warbling sound to attract nearby pups and then smells and touches them to find the one that belongs to her.

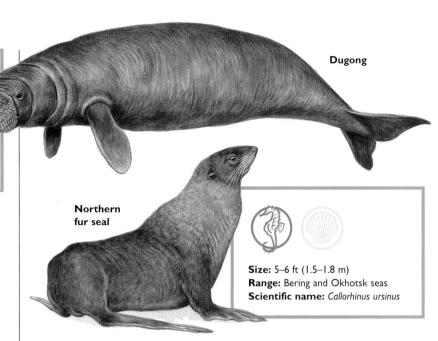

Dugong

Size: up to 10 ft (3 m)
Range: Red Sea, Indian Ocean, and waters off northern Australia
Scientific name: *Dugong dugon*

Dugong

Surprisingly dugongs and manatees are related to elephants. The dugong is fleshy yet streamlined, with a crescent-shaped tail. It is shy and solitary, spending much of its life on the seabed feeding on seaweed and seagrass. A female dugong gives birth to a single baby and helps it to the surface to breathe.

American manatee

Manatees live in estuaries, bays, and shallow coastal waters. They are good swimmers and can reach speeds of 16 mph (25 km/h). They use their flattened tails as paddles and sometimes walk along the bottom of the ocean on their flippers, grazing on seagrass.

Northern fur seal

Size: 5–6 ft (1.5–1.8 m)
Range: Bering and Okhotsk seas
Scientific name: *Callorhinus ursinus*

Northern fur seal

Northern fur seals have larger rear flippers than other sea lions. Both males and females have a pale patch on the neck, but the male may be up to four times the female's weight. These fur seals feed on fish and squid, alone or in pairs, and rarely come to land outside the breeding season. Males establish territories on the breeding beaches before females arrive to give birth to their young.

Australian sea lion

This sea lion, which does not migrate, never travels far from the beach where it was born. It moves easily on land despite its bulk and may travel several miles onshore. It comes onto land often throughout the year. Fish, squid, and penguins are its main foods. This species is usually found in small groups. The males establish territories, which they defend fiercely.

American manatee

Size: up to 10 ft (3 m)
Range: Atlantic and Caribbean coastal waters from southeastern United States to Brazil
Scientific name: *Trichechus manatus*

Size: up to 7¾ ft (2.4 m)
Range: off south and southwest Australia
Scientific name: *Neophoca cinerea*

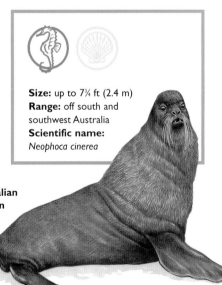

Australian sea lion

Waders and waterbirds

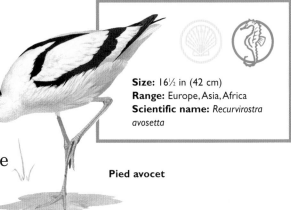

Size: 16½ in (42 cm)
Range: Europe, Asia, Africa
Scientific name: *Recurvirostra avosetta*

Pied avocet

Waders live in wetlands or coastal environments. They can be identified by their long bills, which they use to pick out small invertebrates from mud or soil. Different species have different length bills so that they do not compete with each other for food. Waterbirds are able to swim, float on the water, and even dive in shallow water. They have webbed feet and flat bills. Their feathers contain a special oil that makes them almost waterproof.

Pied avocet

The avocet has an unusual long beak that curves upward. It catches insects and small water creatures by holding its beak slightly open and sweeping it from side to side on the surface of mud or in shallow water. In deeper water, it dips its head below the surface to find food.

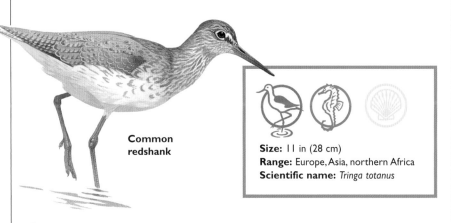

Common redshank

Size: 11 in (28 cm)
Range: Europe, Asia, northern Africa
Scientific name: *Tringa totanus*

Eurasian oystercatcher

The oystercatcher has a long, blunt beak, which it uses to pry shellfish such as cockles and mussels off seaside rocks and then to chisel open their shells. It also eats insects and worms, which it finds on farmland.

Common redshank

This bird lives near almost any kind of water. It breeds on moorland and marshes but spends the winter on shores, mud flats, meadows, and estuaries. Insects are its main food, but it also eats other small creatures such as crabs and snails. It lays eggs in a grass-lined nest on the ground.

Eurasian oystercatcher

Size: 18 in (46 cm)
Range: coastal Europe, coastal Siberia, central Russia
Scientific name: *Haematopus ostralegus*

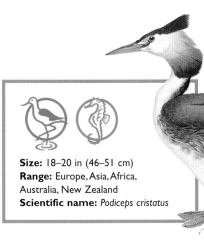

Great crested grebe

Size: 18–20 in (46–51 cm)
Range: Europe, Asia, Africa, Australia, New Zealand
Scientific name: *Podiceps cristatus*

Great crested grebe

This beautiful bird does not often fly, and it is rarely seen on land, where it moves awkwardly. Before mating, great crested grebes perform an elegant courtship dance on the water. During the dance they wag their heads and present each other with pieces of weed.

Common eider

Like most ducks the common eider lines her nest with downy feathers plucked from her own breast. The down of the eider is particularly warm and soft. It has long been collected by people for filling items such as comforters and sleeping bags. Eiders live mainly on shellfish and other small creatures.

Size: 22–28 in (56–71 cm)
Range: the far north of Europe and North America
Scientific name: *Somateria mollissima*

Common eider

Red-throated loon

This graceful bird has a slender beak and a red patch on its throat. It flies well and can take off easily from the water. An expert swimmer, it feeds on fish that it catches underwater. It makes a variety of calls, including growling sounds and high-pitched wails. The female lays two eggs in a nest on the ground or in shallow water.

Red-throated loon

Size: 20–27 in (53–69 cm)
Range: North America, northern Asia, northern Europe
Scientific name: *Gavia stellata*

Greater flamingo

The flamingo's long legs allow it to wade into deeper water than most other birds when looking for food. It feeds by sucking water and mud in at the front of its beak and then pumping it out again at the sides, where comblike bristles trap small plants and animals. The flamingo builds a nest of mud, where it usually lays only one egg.

Size: 3½–4¾ ft (1.1–1.45 m)
Range: southern Europe, parts of Asia and Africa, Mexico, West Indies, Central and South America
Scientific name:
Phoenicopterus ruber

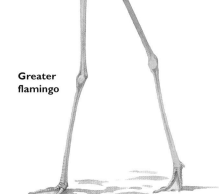

Greater flamingo

Seabirds

Life at sea is demanding for birds. Many, such as albatrosses, gannets, and terns, are strong fliers. They cover long distances over the open ocean as they search for food. Some spend almost the entire year in the air, coming to land only to mate, lay eggs, and raise their chicks. There are some seabirds that cannot fly at all—for example, penguins, which are expert swimmers and divers.

Dovekie

Large numbers of these birds, also known as little auks, live in the Arctic. In summer they breed in colonies of millions on Arctic coasts and cliffs. They can fly, but they also swim and dive well. They feed on small fish and other small creatures, such as shellfish.

Dovekie

Size: 7¾ in (20 cm)
Range: Arctic and north Atlantic oceans and the Bering Sea
Scientific name: *Alle alle*

Snowy sheathbill

These birds are scavengers. They haunt penguin colonies to seize eggs and chicks, and raid the garbage dumps of Antarctic research stations. They also feed on fish and shellfish. They swim and fly but spend most of their time on the ground.

Size: 15½ in (39 cm)
Range: Antarctic coasts and south Atlantic islands
Scientific name: *Chionis alba*

Snowy sheathbill

Great cormorant

The cormorant swims using its webbed feet. It eats mainly fish and catches prey during dives that may last as long as a minute. It brings fish to the surface and tosses them in the air to swallow them head first. The cormorant makes a nest in a tree or on the ground. The female lays three or four eggs, and both parents care for the chicks.

Great cormorant

Size: 28–31 in (71–79 cm)
Range: Atlantic coasts of North America and Europe
Scientific name: *Larus marinus*

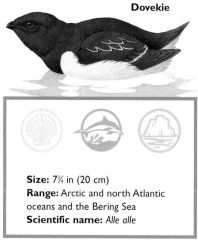

Young great black-backed gull

Great black-backed gull

One of the largest gulls, this bird is a fierce hunter. It kills other seabirds, such as puffins, and takes their eggs and young. It also eats fish and scavenges waste.

Great skua

Size: 20–22 in (51–56 cm)
Range: north Atlantic Ocean
Scientific name: *Catharacta skua*

Great skua

A strong bird with a hooked bill, the great skua attacks other birds to steal their prey, but also kills and eats gulls, puffins, and kittiwakes and preys on their eggs and young. It also eats unwanted fish thrown overboard from fishing boats.

Size: 31½–39½ in (80–100 cm)
Range: coasts of North America, Europe, Africa, Asia, Australia
Scientific name: *Phalacrocorax carbo*

Common tern

A coastal bird, this tern feeds on shrimp and other small sea creatures. It catches its food by hovering above the sea until it spots something and then diving rapidly into the water to seize the prey in its sharp beak. Terns nest in large colonies on islands and cliffs. The female lays two or three eggs in a nest scraped into the ground.

Brown pelican

The brown pelican is the smallest pelican. It feeds by diving for fish, making high-speed plunges into the water from heights of more than 30 feet (9 m). This bird lays two or three eggs in a nest on the ground.

Brown pelican

Size: 4 ft (1.2 m)
Range: Pacific and Atlantic coasts of North and South America
Scientific name: *Pelecanus occidentalis*

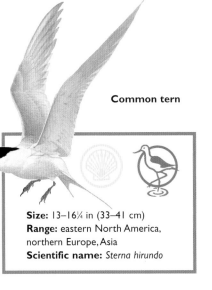
Common tern

Size: 13–16¼ in (33–41 cm)
Range: eastern North America, northern Europe, Asia
Scientific name: *Sterna hirundo*

Herring gull

This is the most common gull on North American and European sea coasts. It catches small fish, steals eggs and young from other birds, and scavenges waste. It also flies inland to find worms and other creatures. Herring gulls make nests of weeds and grass on cliffs, beaches, or rooftops. The female lays two or three eggs, which are cared for by both parents.

Herring gull

Size: 21¾–26 in (55–66 cm)
Range: most of northern hemisphere
Scientific name: *Larus argentatus*

Little (fairy) penguin

Little (fairy) penguin

The smallest of all the penguins, this penguin lives around coasts and islands, looking for small fish and other food in shallow waters. It nests in a crevice or burrow. The female lays two eggs, which both parents take turns incubating for between 33 and 40 days.

Size: 15¾ in (40 cm) tall
Range: New Zealand and southern Australia
Scientific name: *Eudyptula minor*

Jackass penguin

This penguin lives in a warmer climate than most other penguins, but keeps cool in the cold offshore current. It breeds on land and nests in a burrow or under rocks. It is active on land only at night.

Galápagos penguin

This is the only penguin that lives near the equator. The Galápagos Islands are bathed by a cool current, making the area suitable for a cold-loving penguin. The Galápagos penguin feeds mainly on small fish. It nests in small groups, and females lay two eggs in a cave or a hole in volcanic rock.

Jackass penguin

Size: 27¼ in (69 cm) tall
Range: South Africa
Scientific name: *Spheniscus demersus*

Size: 19¾ in (50 cm) tall
Range: Galápagos Islands
Scientific name: *Spheniscus mendiculus*

Galápagos penguin

Size: 3½–4½ ft (1.1–1.35 m)
Range: southern oceans
Scientific name: *Diomedea exulans*

Wandering albatross

This seabird has the longest wingspan of any bird—up to 11 feet (3.4 m). It spends most of its life soaring over the open ocean, sometimes flying up to 300 miles (500 km) in a day.

Red-tailed tropicbird

This elegant seabird is an expert in the air but moves awkwardly on land. It usually nests on ledges or cliffs in a position that allows for easy takeoff. Fish and squid are its main food. Females lay a single egg on the ground. Both parents incubate the egg and care for the chick.

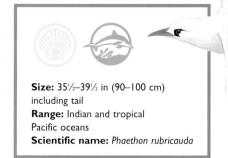

Size: 35½–39½ in (90–100 cm) including tail
Range: Indian and tropical Pacific oceans
Scientific name: *Phaethon rubricauda*

Wandering albatross

Atlantic puffin

Atlantic puffin

This puffin uses its colorful beak to catch fish and can hold as many as a dozen fish at a time. An expert swimmer and diver, the puffin can also fly well. Its short legs are set well back on the body, so it waddles clumsily when it comes on land to nest. The female puffin lays one egg, sometimes two, in an old burrow or in a new hole.

Size: 11–14 in (29–36 cm)
Range: north Atlantic Ocean
Scientific name: *Fratercula arctica*

Great frigatebird

This large seabird has a wingspan of more than 6 feet (1.8 m) and a big, hooked beak. It spends most of its life in the air. It catches food by snatching prey from the surface of the water or by threatening other seabirds until they drop their meals. Large colonies nest together on oceanic islands.

Size: 34–39 in (86–100 cm)
Range: Indian and Pacific oceans
Scientific name:
Fregata minor

European storm-petrel

This seabird eats fish and squid, which it catches as it swoops low over the water. It also eats food scraps thrown from ships. The storm-petrel spends most of its life at sea but comes ashore in the breeding season to nest in a burrow or rock crevice.

European storm-petrel

Size: 5½–7 in (14–18 cm)
Range: northeastern Atlantic Ocean to the Mediterranean
Scientific name: *Hydrobates pelagicus*

Northern gannet

A sturdily built seabird with a strong beak, the northern gannet soars over the ocean, searching for fish and squid. When it spots prey, the gannet plunges 100 feet (30 m) or more into the water to seize the catch and bring it to the surface.

Northern gannet

Size: 34–39 in (87–100 cm)
Range: north Atlantic Ocean to the Gulf of Mexico
Scientific name: *Morus bassanus*

Red-tailed tropicbird

Great frigatebird

Penguins

Penguins (see also p.88) are better suited to life in the sea than any other bird. They are expert swimmers and divers, using their strong flippers to push themselves through the water. On land, penguins walk upright and have an awkward gait. They cannot fly. Most penguins live in the Antarctic and on islands near the Antarctic Circle, and have to survive in freezing conditions. They have a dense covering of waterproof feathers, which keeps them both warm and dry. A thick layer of fat beneath the feathers also helps to keep out the cold. There are 17 species of penguins. The smallest is the little, or fairy, penguin, which measures about 15 inches (39 cm). The biggest is the emperor penguin, which is about 3¾ feet (1.15 m) tall. All have similar coloring, with black or gray feathers on the back and white ones on the belly.

Friendly behavior

Penguins are sociable birds and usually live in huge colonies. Penguins usually keep the same mate for several years. When a breeding pair meets, they rub their heads in greeting. They also preen each other's feathers.

Underwater hunter

The king penguin dives deep to catch prey, often plunging to 150 feet (45 m) or more. The deepest recorded dive for this bird is 820 feet (250 m). The penguin uses its tail and webbed feet for steering as it dives.

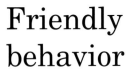

Squid and fish are the main food of the king penguin and other large penguins, such as the emperor. Smaller penguins, such as the gentoos and chinstraps, catch krill and other small sea animals.

Tobogganing

Not at their best on land,
penguins slip and slide
as they waddle on
webbed feet over the
frozen ground. Often the birds
lie down on their bellies and
toboggan over the ice, which is an easier
way to move. Once in the water, most penguins
swim at speeds of 3 to 6 mph (5 to 10 km/h).

Taking care
of young

At the beginning of winter, the
female emperor penguin lays one
egg on land. Her partner then
incubates the egg on top of his feet
for about 64 days. When the chick
hatches, he keeps it warm on his
feet, tucked under a fold of skin.

Adélie penguins nest in large colonies
along the Antarctic coasts. Eggs are
laid in late November (the Antarctic
spring) and incubated first by the
male and then by the female for a
total of 35 days.

Glossary

ALGAE Plantlike organisms that usually live in water

BARBELS Thin, whiskerlike projections found on the lip area of some species of fish. They are primarily used to locate food.

BALEEN Literally means "whalebone;" also used to describe species of whales that have whalebone plates instead of teeth. These baleen plates can be used to filter tiny animals—such as krill—from the water.

BIOLUMINESCENCE The natural production of light by some species of fish, because the ocean where they live is too dark

BRACHIOPOD Invertebrate species of marine life that has shells which are made up of two parts hinged together

CAMOUFLAGE Colors or patterns on an animal that make it blend into its background

CNIDARIAN A group of invertebrate organisms, the majority of which live in the oceans. They include corals and jellyfish.

DORSAL FIN The vertical fin along the back of a fish

ECHOLOCATION A process for determining the location of objects, such as animals, using sound waves that are then reflected back to the sender

ESTUARY The mouth of a river

EUTHERIAN Mammal whose live young grow inside the mother's womb until she gives birth

FRESH WATER The type of water found in rivers and lakes, rather than salty sea water

GILLS The organs, often resembling flaps, used by fish to absorb oxygen from the water into their blood

INCUBATE To keep eggs warm until they are ready to hatch into young

INVERTEBRATE Animal without a backbone. An invertebrate can live on land, in sea water, in fresh water, and even in the air.

MIGRATION Long journey made, often yearly, by animals in order to breed or to find food

PARASITE Organism living directly on another organism and getting nourishment from the host creature

PECTORAL FINS The fins on a fish that act in the same way as the arms or front legs of a four-legged animal

PLANKTON The microscopic plants and animals that float near the surface of seas and lakes

PHYTOPLANKTON Plant plankton

POLYP A small, invertebrate sea-dwelling animal. A coral polyp forms a hard, protective shell out of calcium carbonate. When the polyp dies, the chalky skeleton remains, and another polyp will grow on top of the old one, forming a coral reef.

SCHOOL The collective term for a group of fish

SPAWN To produce, or lay, eggs

VERTEBRATE Animal with a backbone

ZOOPLANKTON Animal plankton

Index

Acknowledgments

PHOTOGRAPHIC CREDITS

t= top; b= bottom; l= left; r= right

8t Wolfgang Kaehler/Corbis; 8c Paul Steel/The Stock Market; 12–13 David B. Fleetham/ Oxford Scientific Films; 35 Richard Herrmann/Oxford Scientific Films; 45 Peter Parks/ Oxford Scientific Films; 52 Jeffrey L. Rotman/Corbis; 53l Robert Yin/Corbis; 53t Louise Murrey/Robert Harding Picture Library; 66t MD/Corbis; 66b Galeen Rowell/Corbis; 72–73 Paul A. Souders/Corbis; 75 Jeff Foott/BBC Natural History Unit; 81 Rick Price/ Oxford Scientific Films; 91 Colin Monteath/Oxford Scientific Films.

ARTWORK CREDITS

Graham Allen, Robin Boutell, Keith Brewer, Hilary Burn, Joanne Cowne, Sandra Doyle, Malcolm Ellis, John Francis, Elizabeth Gray, Terry Hadler, Gary Hincks, Bridget James, Elizabeth Kay, Steve Kirk, Adrian Lascom, Alan Male, Colin Newman, Chris Orr, Denys Ovenden, Steve Roberts, Bernard Robinson, Eric Robson, Peter D. Scott, Guy Smith, Roger Stewart, Simon Turvey, Dick Twinney, Ken Wood, Michael Woods, Colin Woolf. Habitat icons: Roy Flooks.